ainsley harriott's meals in minutes

BBC BOOKS

ainsley
harriott's
meals
in minutes

BBC BOOKS

All eggs used in the recipes are medium sized.
All vegetables except new potatoes should be peeled unless the
recipe says otherwise.

This book is published to accompany the television series entitled *Meals in Minutes* which
was first broadcast in 1998. The series was produced by Bazal for the BBC.

Executive Producer: Linda Clifford
Producer: Caroline Officer

Published by BBC Books
an imprint of BBC Worldwide Limited
80 Wood Lane
London
W12 0TT

First published 1998
© Ainsley Harriott 1998
The moral right of the author has been asserted.

ISBN 0 563 38427 1

Recipes developed and written in association with Silvana Franco.
Studio Photographs by Juliet Piddington © BBC
Location photographs by Craig Easton © BBC
Remaining studio photographs by Roger Stowell for *BBC Good Food Magazine* © Roger Stowell.

Some of the recipes and photographs in this publication have been featured
in *BBC Good Food Magazine* in their monthly feature,
Ainsley Harriott's Meals in Minutes.

Commissioning Editor: Nicky Copeland
Editors: Kate Quarry and Rachel Brown
Art Editor: Jane Coney
Design by Town Group Creative
Home Economist for Juliet Piddington: Sarah Ramsbottom
Home Economists for Roger Stowell: Vicky Musselman and Angela Nilsen

Set in Trade Gothic Condensed and Franklin Gothic by Town Group Creative.
Printed and bound in Great Britain by Butler and Tanner Ltd, Frome.
Colour origination by Radstock Reproductions Ltd, Midsomer Norton.
Jacket printed by Lawrence Allen Ltd, Weston-super-Mare.

contents

Believe me, once you've tried *Meals in Minutes* your enthusiasm for good, simple nosh becomes more and more infectious. You'll be able to boogie into your kitchen knowing that whatever is hanging around can be quickly whipped into a gourmet feast. Food shopping will be done with confidence invaluable if you're stretched for time – just think, you'll be able to pick up a few vital elements, fresh or ready-made, knowing that they'll combine beautifully with all those bits of capital you've got at home.

Now, just because food is cooked in minutes instead of hours doesn't mean you have to compromise on great taste and presentation – even with classics like Coq au Vin or Cassoulet, or, indeed, my 20-minute Peking Duck. They all look fabulous and taste wonderful. Perhaps you're looking for a complete roast dinner in less than an hour, or stunning snacks in five minutes flat. Yes, there's not a lot you can do in five minutes in the kitchen is there? Feeling sceptical? How's about breathtaking dazzling desserts like my Zapped Lemon Curd Pudding and my Choco-nana Brandy Snaps, both ready in less than twelve minutes?

introduction

So . . . why meals in minutes? Well, the amount of times people have come up to me, especially in supermarkets, occasionally in the dry cleaner's, now and then in the florist's and also in the Gent's, and asked me to recommend a delicious recipe that can be knocked up in minutes rather than hours is quite staggering! I discovered that these people all had something in common: some worked strange shifts, some were loaded with children, but generally it was a case of working hard and playing hard, yet everyone wanted to eat fantastic home-cooked food in a flash. So, I wanted to write a book and make a television series that would hopefully give them food for thought and answer all those culinary conundrums. And here it is!

Believe me, once you get into *Meals in Minutes* your enthusiasm for good, simple nosh becomes more and more infectious. You'll be able to bounce into your kitchen knowing that whatever is hanging around can be quickly whipped into a gourmet feast. Food shopping will be done with confidence – invaluable if you're stretched for time. Just think, you'll be able to pick up a few ingredients, fresh or ready-made, knowing that they'll combine beautifully with all those store-cupboard goodies at home.

Now, just because food is cooked in minutes instead of hours doesn't mean you have to compromise on great taste and presentation – even with classics like my Coq au Vin or Cassoulet, or, indeed, my 20-minute Peking Duck. They all look fabulous and taste wonderful. Perhaps you're looking for a complete roast dinner in less than an hour, or stunning snacks in five minutes flat. Yes, there's not a lot you can do in five minutes in the kitchen is there? Feeling smart? How's about breathtaking dazzling desserts like my Zapped Lemon Curd Pudding or my Choco-nana Brandy Snaps, both ready in less than twelve minutes? Oooh you lucky people. Go on, get into meals in minutes, discover the art of the perfect store-cupboard, lots of brilliant kitchen tips and fast, fabulous food.

Enjoy!

time-saving ideas

While most of us aspire to a tasty, varied and nutritious diet, in most of our hectic lives, time is of the essence when it comes to getting down to business in the kitchen. To help save your energy and get the most out of your time spent at the stove, I've come up with a few handy tips that I always bear in mind when cooking for my own family.

Make your kitchen comfortable

From good lighting to uncluttered work surfaces, in order to get the most out of your cooking you've got to have a pleasant environment in which to work. I always have music on when I'm cooking – yeah, okay – and sometimes a bit of TV, too . . . but if you're enjoying cooking, it will show in the food you create.

Keep it tidy

Do try to keep your kitchen tidy – I always keep equipment I know I'm going to use often, such as my food processor, close to hand and other items such as my electric juicer tucked away ready for when I do need to use them. It also saves you lots of time in the long run if you wash up as you go along. Never leave the washing-up until after you've eaten the meal; instead try to clear up as much as possible before you go to sit down and save yourself the hassle of dealing with it all later.

Sort out your store-cupboard

Keep your store-cupboard tidy – regularly throw out items that are out of date and arrange things logically. I always put little stickers on the top of my jars of herbs and spices so I can find what I want without having to rifle through every single jar. As we all know, the one you're looking for is normally the last one you find.

Get the right tools for the job

Ensuring that you've got the right equipment saves you a heck of a lot of time. This is a good example: if you want to mash potatoes, then get a good, solid potato masher; don't try doing it with a flimsy, plastic little number or, worse still, a fork! – it takes all day! Better still, invest in an electric beater – they make the best mash ever. And as for knives, buy good ones and keep them sharp; they're much safer to use and get the chopping done a lot more efficiently. See Equip Yourself on pages 12–13 for more information.

Preparing meals in advance

Many of the dishes in this book can be cooked in advance and then simply reheated. Others can be prepared ahead and just need to be cooked when you're ready to eat. Take the time to plan what you're going to cook and prepare as much as you can as far ahead as possible – you'll save yourself time and worries later.

Making the most of convenience foods

Convenience foods are out there to make our lives easier – make the most of them (see pages 10–11 for more information).

Make double and freeze half

It's well worth making double quantities of suitable dishes then freezing half – it doesn't take all that much longer and you know that you've got a tasty, nutritious meal ready if you just haven't got time to cook.

Use the services on offer

Ask your butcher to dice your meat or bone out your leg of lamb for you and get your fishmonger to fillet, skin and bone your fish – they're there to help you, so make good use of their skills and save yourself a lot of time.

getting stocked up

One of the best-kept secrets of the clever cook's success is a well-stocked larder. From basic essentials such as milk and eggs to the latest in convenience foods such as Mexican flour tortillas – if you keep yourself as well stocked as I am, you'll never run short of ideas when it comes to knocking up a tasty meal in minutes. Of course, there are lots of items in my store-cupboard, some of which just may not be your cup of tea, so either avoid them or swap them for similar items you prefer – after all, cookery is all about experimentation.

Store-cupboard essentials

Canned foods

chopped plum tomatoes
sweetcorn
baked beans
chick peas
red kidney beans
coconut milk
tuna
anchovies
black olives
pimentos (sweet red peppers)
custard
sliced fruit in natural juice

Bottles and jars

sunflower oil, for everyday frying
extra virgin olive oil, for
    salad dressings
sesame oil, for stir-fries and
    Oriental-style dishes
white wine vinegar and
    balsamic vinegar
soy sauce
wholegrain and Dijon mustard
tomato ketchup
Worcestershire sauce
Tabasco or other chilli sauce
curry paste
pesto sauce
sun-dried tomato paste
black olive paste (tapenade)
mayonnaise
crunchy peanut butter
Marmite
clear honey
jam
vanilla extract
wine: red and white
sherry or port
brandy

Dried goods

English mustard powder
baking powder
bicarbonate of soda
small packet plain flour
small packet self-raising flour
cornflour
spaghetti
pasta shapes such as penne or rigatoni
egg noodles
rice: long grain, basmati and risotto
couscous
sugar: caster, light muscovado, icing
stock cubes
herbs and spices: oregano, black
   peppercorns, ground cumin, paprika,
   cayenne, dried chilli flakes, curry powder
   or paste
dried fruit: raisins/sultanas, apricots/prunes
nuts: flaked almonds, unsalted peanuts
bread/pizza dough mix

In the fridge

milk
eggs
unsalted butter
spreadable butter
double cream, crème fraîche or Greek yogurt
soft cheese or mascarpone
Parmesan
mature Cheddar
streaky bacon

Groceries

salad onions
tomatoes
garlic
onions
potatoes
oranges and lemons
bread: take your pick from the incredible
   range now available – I like to use soft
   flour tortillas, standard sliced bread and
   longer-life part-baked breads,
    such as Italian ciabatta

In the freezer

As well as buying ready-frozen items, I like to freeze a lot of my own stuff, too.

root ginger: peel 2.5 cm (1 in) pieces of root ginger, cover in freezer film and freeze –
it's much easier to grate when frozen and means you'll always have a supply handy

herbs: any left-over fresh herbs can be packed in strong plastic bags and stored in the
freezer – they're really good for cooking with and when you need to use them, just pull
off a handful and crumble them into your pan – no need to chop!

bread: most bread freezes very well

garden peas
leaf spinach
vanilla ice cream
ready-rolled puff pastry

equip yourself

Make life easier for yourself by getting well equipped – you don't need a lot of gear, but it makes sense if you buy the best that you can afford: then you know it'll work for you and last longer than a cheaper counterpart. It is also very important if you are opting for cheaper equipment to ensure that it is safe – avoid any flimsy equipment and make sure that saucepans and knives have strong handles.

Here's a list of basic equipment that you would do well to stock up on – and don't forget, each piece you buy should be treated as an investment, as many high-quality items have very long guarantees.

The basics

1 large sharp knife
1 small sharp knife
1 chef's steel/knife
   sharpener
can opener
2 chopping boards
large frying pan
3 sizes of saucepan
   with lids
3 wooden spoons
set of kitchen scales
colander
measuring jug
metal hand whisk
metal sieve
slotted spoon
fish slice

potato masher
swivel-style vegetable
   peeler
box-style cheese
   grater
pastry brush
rolling pin
roasting tin
baking sheet
casserole dish with lid

Handy extras

As well as the essentials,
here's a list of items that
will often prove pretty handy
in the kitchen.

lemon zester
tongs
potato ricer
palette knife
hand-held blender
food processor
garlic press
wok
rubber spatula
lemon juicer
tea strainer
flour dredger

soups, snacks, salads

chicken and sweetcorn soup

A popular soup traditionally from the southwest of China. It's deliciously easy to make and thoroughly heart-warming. You can also try making it with a tin of creamed sweetcorn – if so, leave out the cornflour, as it's already quite thick.

SERVES 2 | PREPARATION: 5 MINS | COOKING TIME: 15 MINS

1 tablespoon vegetable oil
1 x 100 g (4 oz) skinless, boneless chicken breast, finely diced
1 garlic clove, finely chopped
1 cm (½ in) piece root ginger, finely chopped
1 tablespoon cornflour
600 ml (1 pint) hot chicken stock
100 g (4 oz) sweetcorn kernels
1 egg
1 tablespoon fresh lemon juice
shredded salad onions, to garnish
dark soy sauce and prawn crackers, to serve
toasted sesame seeds to garnish

Heat the oil in a deep pan and gently cook the chicken, garlic and ginger for 3–4 minutes without colouring.

Blend the cornflour with a little stock and add to the soup pan with the remaining stock and the sweetcorn. Bring to the boil, stirring continuously, and simmer gently for 5–7 minutes.

Beat together the egg and lemon juice and slowly trickle into the soup pan, stirring with a chopstick or fork to make egg strands. Season to taste, garnish with salad onions and toasted sesame seeds, and serve with a drizzle of soy sauce and some prawn crackers.

NUTRITION NOTES PER SERVING: calories 271 | protein 17 g | carbohydrate 23.6 g fat 12.8 g | saturated fat 2.26 g | fibre 0.8 g | added sugar 3.37 g | salt 1.52 g

clam chowder with parmesan croutons

Clam chowder is often thought of as a luxurious dish, but this is very easy to make and uses canned clams, which are widely available from supermarkets.

SERVES 4 | **PREPARATION: 15 MINS | COOKING TIME: 15 MINS**

25 g (1 oz) butter
4 rashers smoked streaky bacon,
  cut into 1 cm (½ in) wide strips
1 onion, finely chopped
1 teaspoon chopped fresh rosemary
  or ¼ teaspoon dried rosemary
225 g (8 oz) floury potatoes, diced
300 ml (10 fl oz) milk
150 ml (5 fl oz) double cream
100 g (4 oz) cod fillet, diced
290 g (10½ oz) can clams in brine

2 tablespoons chopped
  fresh parsley
salt and pepper

FOR THE CROUTONS
2 thick slices country-style bread
2 tablespoons
  freshly grated Parmesan
1 crushed garlic clove
2 tablespoons olive oil

Heat the butter in a small pan and gently cook the bacon, onion and rosemary for 6–7 minutes until softened and golden.

Meanwhile, place the potatoes in a pan with the milk and cream and cook gently for 10–15 minutes until tender.

Pre-heat the oven to 220°C/425°F/gas 7. To make the croutons, cut the bread into large dice and toss with the Parmesan, garlic, olive oil and plenty of seasoning. Scatter onto a baking sheet and roast in the oven for 5–8 minutes, turning occasionally until crisp and golden brown.

Using a potato masher, gently crush the potatoes into the cream mixture, but take care not to over-mash; there should still be several chunks of potato in the soup. Stir in the bacon mixture, the cod and the clams, including the liquid in the can. Simmer very gently for 3–4 minutes until the cod is cooked.

Season to taste and stir in the chopped parsley. Ladle into bowls and scatter over the Parmesan croutons.

NUTRITION NOTES PER SERVING: calories 589 | protein 23.3 g | carbohydrate 31.8 g fat 41.8 g | saturated fat 21.21 g | fibre 1.5 g | added sugar none | salt 3.24 g

snappy zapped stuffed tatties

If you want crispy potato skins, pop them under a hot grill briefly after you've microwaved them, then cut a cross in the top of each, squeeze them up carefully, add the sensationally easy-to-make topping and enjoy.

SERVES 4 | **PREPARATION: 10 MINS | COOKING TIME: 15 MINS**

4 x 250 g (9 oz) baking potatoes, unpeeled
8 rashers smoked streaky bacon, roughly chopped
2 leeks, cut into thin strips
6 salad onions, sliced
100 g (4 oz) full-fat soft cheese
salt and pepper
4 tablespoons soured cream and cayenne pepper, to serve

Scrub, dry and prick the potatoes with a fork. Arrange well apart on a double sheet of kitchen paper. Cook in a microwave on PL9/high for 6 minutes, then turn and cook for a further 6–7 minutes until tender. Allow to stand for 2 minutes. If you don't have a microwave, cook for 1 hour at 220°C/425°F/gas 7 in a preheated oven – longer if you want crispy skins.

Meanwhile, cook the bacon in a non-stick frying pan for 3–4 minutes until crisp. Add the leeks and salad onions and stir-fry for a few minutes until wilted. Add the soft cheese and stir until it melts. Remove from the heat and season to taste with salt and pepper.

Cut a cross in the top of each potato, gently squeeze the base to open out, then pile the filling into the centre. Serve topped with a dollop of soured cream and a sprinkling of cayenne pepper.

NUTRITION NOTES PER SERVING: calories 506 | protein 13 g | carbohydrate 45 g
fat 31 g | saturated fat 16 g | fibre 4 g | added sugar none | salt 2.03 g

clare's chilli bean ranch pasties

These really are packed full of flavour and the kids just love 'em – so does the wife, Clare, too.

SERVES 4   **PREPARATION: 15 MINS | COOKING TIME: 20 MINS**

1 tablespoon sunflower oil
4 rashers smoked streaky bacon, cut into strips
1 small onion, finely chopped
1 garlic clove, finely chopped
200 g (7 oz) can baked beans
50 g (2 oz) mature Cheddar, finely diced
a few drops of Tabasco sauce
375 g (13 oz) pack ready-rolled puff pastry
milk, for brushing
mixed leaf salad, to serve

Pre-heat the oven to 220°C/450°F/gas 7. Heat the oil in a small pan and cook the bacon, onion and garlic for 4–5 minutes until golden. Remove from the heat and mix with the baked beans and diced cheese; add Tabasco to taste.

Open out the pastry and cut into quarters to give four 20 x 11 cm (8 x 4½in) rectangles. Spoon the filling into the centre of each, then bring up the edges to enclose the filling. Press the edges together to create a seam across the centre of each pasty. Transfer to a baking sheet, brush with a little milk and bake for 12–15 minutes until puffed and golden brown.

Serve with salad and watch them disappear.

NUTRITION NOTES PER SERVING: calories 580 | protein 15.1 g | carbohydrate 44.1 g
fat 39.4 g | saturated fat 7.09 g | fibre 2.2 g | added sugar 1.7 g | salt 2.58 g

caramelized tuna tatties

Dress up baked potatoes with mini mountains of rich golden onions, tuna, feta cheese and grilled cherry tomatoes. Just the description gets my juices flowing.

SERVES 2 | **PREPARATION: 5 MINS | COOKING TIME: 20 MINS**

2 x 250 g (9 oz) baking potatoes, unpeeled
10 cherry tomatoes
15 g (½ oz) butter
1 tablespoon olive oil
1 large onion, thinly sliced
85 g (3¼ oz) can tuna in brine, drained
120 g (4½ oz) feta cheese, cubed
salt and pepper

Scrub and dry the potatoes, then prick several times with a fork. Place well apart on a double sheet of kitchen paper; then microwave on PL9/high for 6 minutes. Turn and cook for a further 6–7 minutes until tender. Allow to stand for 2 minutes. If you don't have a microwave, cook for 1 hour at 220°C/425°F/gas 7 in a preheated oven – longer if you want crispy skins.

Pre-heat the grill to high. Place the potatoes and tomatoes on a baking sheet and grill for 4–5 minutes until the potato skins crisp up and the tomatoes just begin to split; keep warm.

Meanwhile, melt the butter with the oil in a small pan and cook the onion for 10 minutes, stirring occasionally until softened and golden. Stir in the tuna and cook for 2–3 minutes to warm through; season to taste.

Cut a deep cross in the top of each potato and squeeze the base gently to open them up. Fill with the tuna mixture then top with the grilled tomatoes and feta; season to taste and serve immediately.

NUTRITION NOTES PER SERVING: calories 426 | protein 22.2 g | carbohydrate 42.9 g fat 19.7 g | saturated fat 11.92 g | fibre 4.7 g | added sugar none | salt 2.97 g

SOUPS | SNACKS | SALADS

22

crispy batton bacon potato cakes

These soft, fluffy potato cakes are great any time of day or night but I love to eat them topped with a fried egg – owright, and a tin of baked beans – for the perfect lazy breakfast.

SERVES 4   **PREPARATION: 10 MINS | COOKING TIME: 25 MINS**

500 g (1 lb 2 oz) floury potatoes, diced
1 tablespoon olive oil
4 rashers smoked streaky bacon, cut into 2 cm (¾ in) wide strips
50 g (2 oz) mature Cheddar, grated
1 teaspoon English mustard
4 salad onions, finely chopped
50 g (2 oz) plain flour
a knob of butter
salt and pepper

Cook the potatoes in boiling, salted water for 10–15 minutes until tender.

Heat the oil in a large frying pan and cook the bacon strips for 3–4 minutes until crisp and well browned.

Drain the potatoes and mash well; stir in the crispy bacon, Cheddar, mustard, salad onions, plain flour and plenty of salt and pepper. Shape the mixture into eight even-sized cakes.

Heat the butter in the bacon pan and gently cook the potato cakes for 3–4 minutes on each side until well browned.

NUTRITION NOTES PER SERVING: calories 318 | protein 10.2 g | carbohydrate 31.6 g
fat 17.5 g | saturated fat 7.6 g | fibre 2.1 g | added sugar none | salt 1.39 g

SOUPS | SNACKS | SALADS

ainsley's aubergine supper stacks

A great crunchy veggie supper that looks good, tastes good and, by golly, probably does you good.

SERVES 4 | PREPARATION: 10 MINS | COOKING TIME: 15 MINS

4 x 1 cm (½ in) thick aubergine slices, cut on the diagonal
1 tablespoon plain flour
1 egg, beaten
8 tablespoons fresh white breadcrumbs
2 tablespoons freshly grated Parmesan
1 teaspoon dried thyme
3 tablespoons olive oil, plus extra for drizzling
1 garlic clove, sliced
2 tomatoes, sliced
4 large slices French or Italian bread, cut on the diagonal
100 g (4 oz) Mozzarella, sliced
salt and pepper
mixed salad leaves, to serve

Coat the aubergine slices in the flour, then dip in the egg. Mix together the breadcrumbs, Parmesan and thyme, and use to coat the slices.

Heat the olive oil in a frying pan and cook the garlic for 30 seconds, then remove and discard. Fry the aubergine in the same pan for 5–8 minutes, turning once, until tender and golden; remove and keep warm. Cook the tomatoes briefly in the same pan then remove and keep warm.

Pre-heat the grill to high. Toast the bread on both sides, then drizzle one side with any pan oil or extra olive oil. Lay the cheese on the bread and grill until it starts to melt. On the serving plates arrange the fried tomato slices over the cheese, then top with aubergine. Serve with the mixed salad leaves.

NUTRITION NOTES PER SERVING: calories 454 | protein 18.8 g | carbohydrate 57.2 g
fat 18.4 g | saturated fat 6.06 g | fibre 2.6 g | added sugar none | salt 2.1 g

cheesy cherry tom potato omelette

Eggs must be one of the most convenient foods. They're the ideal friendly fast food that requires hardly any cooking time, so . . . roll up, roll up for this eggy fiesta feast.

SERVES 2 | PREPARATION: 10 MINS | COOKING TIME: 15 MINS

50 g (2 oz) Edam or Mozzarella, grated
4 cherry tomatoes, quartered
4 small cooked new potatoes, sliced
1 tablespoon snipped fresh chives
4 eggs
a knob of butter
½ teaspoon olive oil
salt and pepper

Mix together the grated cheese, tomato quarters, potato slices and snipped chives. Beat together the eggs and a little seasoning in a separate bowl.

Melt the butter and oil in a 23–25 cm (9–10 in) frying pan, then pour in the beaten egg. As the omelette cooks, use a fork to gather the set egg into the centre of the pan so the runny egg can run to the edge to cook. Continue to cook over a low heat for several minutes until just set.

Pre-heat the grill to high. Tilt the pan, then use a spatula to roll up the omelette. Carefully transfer to a warm, heatproof plate ensuring that the join is underneath.

Cut a slit along the top and spoon in the tomato and chive mixture. Place under the grill for 1 minute to melt the cheese and warm the filling. Season with salt and pepper and serve hot.

NUTRITION NOTES PER SERVING: calories 301 | protein 20 g | carbohydrate 11 g fat 20 g | saturated fat 8 g | fibre 1 g | added sugar none | salt 1.58 g

Spice up this dish by sprinkling over a little Worcestershire or Tabasco sauce.

sunny-side hash 'n' ham

This simple, classic dish, topped with fried eggs, will keep your sunny side up.

SERVES 2 | **PREPARATION: 10 MINS | COOKING TIME: 20 MINS**

450 g (1 lb) floury potatoes, diced
2 tablespoons olive oil
1 x 175 g (6 oz) gammon steak, diced
225 g (8 oz) Savoy cabbage, thinly sliced
100 ml (3½ fl oz) vegetable stock
1 tablespoon chopped fresh parsley
2 eggs
salt and pepper

Cook the potatoes in a pan of boiling, salted water for 5–7 minutes until just tender; drain well.

Heat 1 tablespoon of the olive oil in a frying pan and cook the gammon and potatoes for 5 minutes, stirring occasionally, until the potatoes are crisp and golden; remove the gammon and potatoes from the pan and set aside. Stir the cabbage and stock into the same pan and cook for 6–8 minutes until tender; season to taste and stir in the parsley. Return the gammon and potatoes to the pan and keep warm.

Meanwhile, heat the remaining oil in a small non-stick frying pan; crack in the eggs and cook for 3–4 minutes until set.

Divide the potato mixture between two serving plates and top each with a fried egg; season to taste and serve immediately.

NUTRITION NOTES PER SERVING: calories 562 | protein 28.4 g | carbohydrate 39.1 g
fat 33.5 g | saturated fat 9.36 g | fibre 6.3 g | added sugar 0.5 g | salt 3.26 g

melting eggy-bread sandwich

You didn't think eggy bread could get any better, did you? Well, a bit of oozy cheese and some tasty ham make my eggy-bread sandwich just about the most satisfying snack you could ask for.

SERVES 1 | **PREPARATION: 10 MINS | COOKING TIME: 10 MINS**

25 g (1 oz) Gruyère or Mozzarella, grated
1 cherry tomato, roughly diced
1 slice of cooked ham, cut into thin strips
2 fresh basil leaves, roughly torn, or a pinch of dried oregano
2 slices of white bread
1 egg
2 tablespoons milk
1–2 tablespoons olive oil or 25 g (1 oz) butter
salt and pepper

Mix together the cheese, tomato, ham and basil or oregano; season to taste. Sprinkle the mixture over one slice of bread and place the other slice on top, pressing down firmly to make a sandwich.

Beat the egg, milk and a little seasoning together in a shallow dish, lay the sandwich in the mixture and leave to soak for 2–3 minutes. Turn the sandwich over and leave for a further 2–3 minutes until all the liquid has been absorbed.

Heat the olive oil or butter in a large frying pan and gently cook the sandwich for 3–4 minutes on each side until puffed and golden. Drain on kitchen paper and serve immediately.

NUTRITION NOTES PER SERVING: calories 487 | protein 24.5 g | carbohydrate 36.1 g fat 28.2 g | saturated fat 9.48 g | fibre 1.2 g | added sugar none | salt 2.71 g

Don't be tempted to cook the sandwich over too high a heat as it will brown very quickly, before the cheese inside has melted.

SOUPS | SNACKS | SALADS

flashed smoked salmon bagels

Smoked salmon comes ready to eat but I find that a quick flash in the pan changes the texture and offers a deliciously different way to enjoy it. Perhaps it's the creamy, soft egg, runny yolk and charred salmon . . . what do you think?

SERVES 2   PREPARATION: 5 MINS | COOKING TIME: 5 MINS

2 eggs
1 bagel
a small knob of butter
2 slices smoked salmon
2 tablespoons crème fraîche
1 tablespoon snipped fresh chives
salt and pepper

Pre-heat the grill to high. Boil the eggs in a small pan for 4 minutes. Meanwhile, halve the bagel and cook under the hot grill for 1–2 minutes until toasted. Spread with a little butter.

Heat a small non-stick frying pan and when hot cook the smoked salmon slices for 30 seconds on one side only.

Place the toasted bagel halves on two serving plates and ruffle the cooked smoked salmon on top. Spoon over a dollop of crème fraîche. Drain and shell the eggs and place one on top of the crème fraîche, season to taste, sprinkle with chives and serve immediately.

NUTRITION NOTES PER SERVING: calories 338 | protein 24.8 g | carbohydrate 22.7 g
fat 17.1 g | saturated fat 7.48 g | fibre 0.7 g | added sugar none | salt 3.74 g

spiked salad onion supper crêpes

You might find your own favourite filling with enough practice, but this little lot really does the trick. Pancake-packed with crêpe flavours – yes please!

SERVES 4 | **PREPARATION: 10 MINS | COOKING TIME: 15 MINS**

250 g (9 oz) new potatoes, sliced
100 g (4 oz) green beans, sliced
6 rashers rindless streaky
  bacon, chopped
1 small onion, chopped
soured cream and chilli powder,
  to serve
watercress, to garnish

FOR THE CRÊPES
100 g (4 oz) plain flour
a pinch of salt
2 eggs
300 ml (10 fl oz) milk
1 tablespoon vegetable oil,
  plus extra for frying
4 salad onions, finely chopped
2 tablespoons chopped fresh parsley

To make the crêpes beat together the flour, salt and eggs. Gradually beat in the milk to make a smooth batter, then stir in 1 tablespoon of the oil, the salad onions and parsley.

Steam the potatoes over a pan of boiling water for 3 minutes; add the beans and continue to cook for a further 7 minutes until both are tender.

Heat a little vegetable oil in a 20–23 cm (8–9 in) non-stick frying pan, then pour in enough batter to coat the base evenly. Cook for about 2 minutes until golden underneath, then turn and cook for 1 minute; keep warm while you repeat three times with the remaining batter.

Heat a little oil in a frying pan and cook the bacon and onion for 4–5 minutes until golden; add the potatoes and beans and gently warm through.

Fold the crêpes into triangles to make pockets and fill with the bacon mixture. Top each with a spoonful of soured cream and a sprinkling of chilli. Garnish with the watercress and serve.

NUTRITION NOTES PER SERVING: calories 426 | protein 16 g | carbohydrate 39 g
fat 24 g | saturated fat 9 g | fibre 3 g | added sugar none | salt 1.9 g

finger-licking chicken wings

Chicken wings are inexpensive, cook quickly and make fabulous finger food. Try eating these without licking your fingers!

SERVES 4   **PREPARATION: 5 MINS | COOKING TIME: 35 MINS**

1 tablespoon vegetable oil
1 small onion, very finely chopped
2 garlic cloves, crushed
2 tablespoons clear honey
4 tablespoons tomato ketchup
4 tablespoons Worcestershire sauce
2 teaspoons English mustard
2 teaspoons Tabasco sauce
8 chicken wings, tips removed
2 tablespoons flour, seasoned with salt and pepper

Pre-heat the oven to 200°C/400°F/gas 6.

Heat the oil in a small pan and cook the onion and garlic for 3–4 minutes until softened. Stir in the honey, ketchup, Worcestershire sauce, mustard and Tabasco and simmer very gently for a minute or so.

Dust the chicken in the seasoned flour then brush liberally with the sauce. Place on a baking sheet and roast for 30 minutes until well browned and cooked through.

Transfer to a serving plate and keep those napkins handy, or just lick those fingers!

NUTRITION NOTES PER SERVING: calories 440 | protein 24.3 g | carbohydrate 33.1 g
fat 24.4 g | saturated fat 5.69 g | fibre 1.6 g | added sugar 13 g | salt 1.54 g

teasing turkey pitta pockets

You can't beat a good tease when hungry, so for a casual lunchtime or teatime snack you can't go far wrong with my turkey pitta pockets. They'll tease your tastebuds right 'til the last bite.

SERVES 4 | **PREPARATION: 10 MINS | COOKING TIME: 10 MINS**

1 tablespoon vegetable oil
a knob of butter
1 onion, thinly sliced
2 garlic cloves, finely chopped
50 g (2 oz) fresh white breadcrumbs
6 fresh sage leaves, finely chopped
grated rind and juice of 1 lemon
½–1 teaspoon Cajun seasoning or mild chilli powder
200 g (7 oz) cooked turkey, cut into 1 cm (½ in) strips
salt and pepper
4 pitta breads
shredded iceberg or cos lettuce, sliced red onion and 4 tablespoons
    soured cream or Greek yogurt, to serve
wedges of lemon (optional)

Heat the oil and butter in a large frying pan and cook the onion and garlic for 3–4 minutes until softened and golden. Stir in the breadcrumbs, sage, lemon rind, Cajun seasoning and turkey and stir fry for 2–3 minutes until the breadcrumbs begin to brown. Add the lemon juice and season to taste.

Make a slit in the side of each pitta. Mix together the lettuce and red onion and pack into the bottom of each pitta pocket. Pile in the turkey mixture and top with a dollop of soured cream or Greek yogurt and, if you like, a squeeze of lemon juice.

NUTRITION NOTES PER SERVING: calories 414 | protein 23.9 g | carbohydrate 62 g fat 9.5 g | saturated fat 3.01 g | fibre 2.7 g | added sugar none | salt 1.73 g

We like a
bit of that,
don't we?
Yes we do!

honeyed tarragon quick chick salad

I like to cook the chicken on a griddle pan, which gives the chicken lovely markings and a smoky taste, but a frying pan or wok does the job just as well. A bottle or two of iced lager goes down a treat.

SERVES 2 PREPARATION: 15 MINS | COOKING TIME: 5 MINS

3 tablespoons olive oil
grated rind and juice of 1 lemon
1 garlic clove, chopped
1 tablespoon chopped fresh tarragon
2 x 100 g (4 oz) boneless, skinless chicken breasts, each cut into 6–7 slices
1 teaspoon sesame oil
1–2 teaspoons clear honey
1 tablespoon toasted sesame seeds
3 slices Italian-style bread such as foccacia or ciabatta, toasted and halved
salt and pepper
lettuce leaves and watercress, to serve and garnish

In a small bowl, mix together 2 tablespoons of the olive oil, the lemon rind, 1 teaspoon of lemon juice, the garlic, tarragon, and salt and pepper. Rub the mixture over the chicken slices, then cook in a heated griddle, non-stick frying pan or wok, for 4–5 minutes until golden brown.

Meanwhile, make the dressing: mix together the remaining olive oil and lemon juice with the sesame oil, honey and sesame seeds; season with salt and pepper.

Place three pieces of toast on each serving plate and scatter over the lettuce and watercress. Arrange the chicken slices on top, then spoon over the dressing. Garnish with watercress and serve.

NUTRITION NOTES PER SERVING: calories 634 | protein 39 g | carbohydrate 42 g
fat 35 g | saturated fat 6 g | fibre 2 g | added sugar 4 g | salt 1.9 g

peppy's posh potato salad

A simple, snazzy salad that makes a posh sunshine supper for two, and is bound to be a contender for this year's summer favourite. It's delicious served with some crusty garlic bread. 'But, hey, why wait for the summer?' as my late mother Peppy would have said.

SERVES 2 | **PREPARATION: 10 MINS | COOKING TIME 20 MINS**

250 g (9 oz) small new potatoes
75 g (3 oz) green beans
4 salad onions, diagonally sliced
100 g (4 oz) pitted black olives
50 g (2 oz) thinly sliced salami, cut into quarters

FOR THE DRESSING
3 tablespoons olive oil
1 tablespoon white wine vinegar
1 tablespoon chopped fresh mint
2 teaspoons grainy mustard
salt and pepper

Cook the potatoes in a pan of boiling salted water for 15 minutes, then add the beans and cook for a further 3 minutes until tender but still crisp. Cool under running cold water, then drain and leave to cool.

Cut the potatoes into chunks and toss gently in a serving bowl with the salad onions, olives and salami.

Make the dressing: mix together the oil, vinegar, mint and mustard; season to taste. Pour over the potato salad and lightly toss together. Divide between two serving plates and serve.

NUTRITION NOTES PER SERVING: calories 388 | protein 9 g | carbohydrate 23 g fat 30 g | saturated fat 7 g | fibre 4 g | added sugar trace | salt 3.36 g

vegetarian

cheese 'n' onion tarte tatin

We've done it with apples, we've done it with pears, now do it with onions and watch it disappear. Nothing ever tasted this good upside down.

SERVES 4 PREPARATION: 15 MINS | COOKING TIME: 35 MINS

25 g (1 oz) butter
1 tablespoon olive oil
3 large red onions, thinly sliced
2 tablespoons dark muscovado sugar
1 tablespoon balsamic vinegar
120 g (4½ oz) Cheddar, grated
115 g (4 oz) shortcrust pastry, thawed if frozen
mixed salad, to serve

Pre-heat the oven to 200°C/400°F/gas 6. Melt the butter with the oil in a large frying pan and cook the onions, stirring occasionally, for 5–8 minutes until softened. Stir in the sugar and vinegar and cook for a further 2 minutes until the sugar dissolves. Spoon into a 20 cm (8 in) ovenproof pie dish or sandwich-cake tin.

Reserve 25 g (1 oz) of the cheese and sprinkle the rest over the onions. Roll the pastry out to a circle slightly larger than the dish, then press it lightly over the cheese, tucking down the sides. Prick gently with a fork and bake for about 25 minutes until the pastry is golden and the filling bubbles up round the edge.

Set aside for a few minutes, then place a serving plate on top and invert. While still warm, sprinkle over the reserved cheese, cut into wedges and serve with the salad.

NUTRITION NOTES PER SERVING: calories 388 | protein 10 g | carbohydrate 28 g
fat 27 g | saturated fat 14 g | fibre 2 g | added sugar 8 g | salt 0.78 g

spinach and blue cheese tart

When you fancy a quick nibble, there's nothing like a slice of blue cheese tart – hot or cold. It's simply delicious.

SERVES 4 | **PREPARATION: 10 MINS | COOKING TIME: 40 MINS**

50 g (2 oz) butter
1 small onion, finely chopped
1 garlic clove, finely chopped
350 g (12 oz) fresh spinach
5 x 30 cm (12 in) square sheets filo pastry
75 g (3 oz) Stilton
3 eggs
75 g (3 oz) crème fraîche
¼ teaspoon ground nutmeg, plus extra for sprinkling
salt and pepper
fresh mixed salad and new potatoes, to serve

Pre-heat the oven to 180°C/350°F/gas 4.

Lightly grease a 20 x 4 cm (8 x 1½ in) loose-bottomed flan tin. Melt half the butter in a pan and cook the onion and garlic for 5 minutes until softened. Stir in the spinach and cook for a few minutes until wilted. Turn the mixture into a sieve and press well with a wooden spoon to squeeze out any excess liquid.

Melt the remaining butter. Lay one sheet of filo across the base of the tin with the edges slightly overhanging the sides. Brush well with melted butter. Repeat with the remaining sheets, arranging them at different, overlapping angles.

Spoon the spinach into the base of the pastry case then crumble over the Stilton. Beat together the eggs, crème fraîche, nutmeg and salt and pepper. Pour into the pastry case and sprinkle over a little more nutmeg. Bake for 30 minutes until the filling is set and the pastry golden. Cool a little, then carefully remove from the oven and transfer to a baking sheet. Return to the oven for 5 minutes to crisp up the edges of the tart. Serve with salad and new potatoes.

NUTRITION NOTES PER SERVING: calories 396 | protein 14 g | carbohydrate 18.4 g
fat 30 g | saturated fat 16.82 g | fibre 2.2 g | added sugar 0.6 g | salt 1.97 g

VEGETARIAN

medley of mushroom risotto

I love Italian food, and there's not much that can beat a creamy mushroom risotto, especially one served with juicy, garlicky greens. Oh yes, let those juices flow!

SERVES 2 | **PREPARATION: 5 MINS | COOKING TIME: 30 MINS**

15 g (½ oz) dried cep or
porcini mushrooms
300 ml (10 fl oz) boiling water
2 tablespoons olive oil
1 small onion, finely chopped
2 garlic cloves, finely chopped
225 g (8 oz) risotto rice
600 ml (1 pint) vegetable stock
50 g (2 oz) butter
250 g (9 oz) mixed fresh mushrooms
such as flat field, chestnut,
button, porcini

4 tablespoons chopped fresh
flat-leaf parsley
2 tablespoons freshly grated
Parmesan, plus extra to serve
salt and pepper

FOR THE GARLICKY GREENS
2 tablespoons olive oil
2 garlic cloves, finely chopped
250 g (9 oz) fresh spinach or
100 g (4 oz) shredded
spring greens
salt

Place the dried mushrooms in a bowl and pour over the hot water. Keep the stock ready in a pan on a low heat, and have a ladle handy. Heat 1 tablespoon of olive oil in a large saucepan and cook the onion and garlic for 3–4 minutes until softened. Add the rice and cook for a further 1 minute. Keeping the heat fairly high, add a ladle full of hot stock to the rice and stir until it has been absorbed. Continue to ladle in the stock gradually, stirring until it has all been absorbed. Remove the soaked mushrooms from the liquid and add to the risotto. Gradually stir in the soaking liquid and continue to cook until the rice is almost tender and the liquid has been absorbed.

Meanwhile, heat the remaining oil and a knob of the butter in a frying pan and cook the mushrooms over a high heat for 3–4 minutes. Stir the fried mushrooms, parsley, Parmesan and remaining butter into the risotto pan and season to taste; remove from the heat and cover to keep warm. To prepare the greens, heat the oil in a wok or deep frying pan and cook the garlic for 1 minute. Throw in the greens and stir-fry for 1–2 minutes until wilted. Season with salt. Spoon the risotto into serving bowls and pile the wilted greens in the centre. Shave Parmesan on top of the greens and serve. Buon appetito!

NUTRITION NOTES PER SERVING: calories 871 | protein 22 g | carbohydrate 103.1 g fat 44 g | saturated fat 18.27 g | fibre 5.9 g | added sugar none | salt 3.04 g

silvana's pan-fried pizza italiana

If you think making pizza takes loads of time and effort kneading and tossing, then have a go at my little beauty . . . Mamma mia! You're in for a treat!

SERVES 2   **PREPARATION: 15 MINS | COOKING TIME: 25 MINS**

FOR THE TOMATO SAUCE
1 tablespoon olive oil
2 garlic cloves, finely chopped
2 salad onions, finely chopped
200 g (10 oz) can
  chopped tomatoes
a handful fresh basil, roughly torn
1 tablespoon tomato ketchup
salt and pepper
mixed leaf salad, to serve

FOR THE TOPPINGS
1 tablespoon olive oil,
  plus extra for drizzling
100 g (4 oz) button mushrooms,
  thinly sliced

1 garlic clove, finely chopped
1 tablespoon chopped
  fresh parsley
salt and pepper
1 plum tomato, sliced
50 g (2 oz) Mozzarella, sliced
1 teaspoon capers or 1 tablespoon
  pitted black olives

FOR THE DOUGH
225 g (8 oz) self-raising flour
pinch salt
2 tablespoons freshly
  grated Parmesan
150 ml (5 fl oz) warm water
2 tablespoons olive oil

To make the tomato sauce, heat the olive oil in a small pan and cook the garlic and salad onions for 2–3 minutes until softened. Stir in the tomatoes, basil, tomato ketchup and a little seasoning. Bring to the boil and simmer for 5–10 minutes until thickened. To prepare the mushrooms, heat the olive oil in a small frying pan and cook the mushrooms and garlic for 3–4 minutes until softened. Stir in the parsley and season. Pre-heat the grill to medium.

To make the dough sift the flour and salt into a large bowl; stir in the cheese. Make a well in the centre and stir in the water and 1 tablespoon of olive oil to make a soft dough, then roll into a 25 cm (10 in) round. Heat the remaining olive oil in a skillet or ovenproof frying pan and cook the dough for 5–6 minutes until the underside is golden brown. While the dough is cooking, spoon over the tomato sauce and scatter over the toppings. Drizzle over a little olive oil and place the skillet under a medium grill for 3–4 minutes until the top is golden and the base is cooked through. Cut into wedges and serve with lots of leafy salad.

NUTRITION NOTES PER SERVING: calories 739 | protein 22.7 g | carbohydrate 93.2 g
fat 33.2 g | saturated fat 8.51 g | fibre 6 g | added sugar 1 g | salt 2.74 g

bubbling webbed-cheese pasta

We all know how incredibly versatile pasta is, but what you add to it makes all the difference. So . . . for a wonderful, moreish pasta indulge yourself with my webbed cheesy nosh. If you don't have Mozzarella, use Cheddar or Gruyère instead.

SERVES 2 | PREPARATION: 10 MINS | COOKING TIME: 15 MINS

3 tablespoons olive oil
1 orange pepper, cut lengthways
   into thin strips
1 yellow pepper, cut lengthways
   into thin strips
½ teaspoon caster sugar
250 g (9 oz) rigatoni or penne
2 garlic cloves, finely chopped
1 small onion, finely chopped

500g (1 lb 2 oz) carton
   creamed tomatoes
75 g (3 oz) soft cheese
a handful of fresh basil leaves
150 g (5 oz) Mozzarella,
   roughly cut into 1 cm (½ in) cubes
salt and pepper
mixed salad, to serve

Heat 2 tablespoons of olive oil in a large frying pan and add the pepper strips and caster sugar. Cook over a fairly high heat for 10 minutes, stirring regularly until the peppers are very soft and golden brown. Meanwhile, cook the pasta in a large pan of boiling, salted water according to packet instructions, until tender. Drain well and return to the pan. Heat the remaining olive oil in a small pan and cook the garlic and onion for 2–3 minutes until softened. Stir in the creamed tomatoes and the soft cheese, stirring until the cheese melts and the sauce turns pink. Turn the heat to the lowest setting and simmer the sauce very gently. Add salt and pepper to taste.

Stir together the pasta, caramelized peppers and tomato sauce. Roughly tear the basil leaves and stir them into the mixture, then transfer to a heatproof serving dish. Push the cubes of Mozzarella into the pasta, leaving most of them near the surface, grind plenty of black pepper over the top and place under a preheated grill for 3–4 minutes until the cheese is melted and bubbling. Spoon onto serving plates and serve with a crisp, green salad.

NUTRITION NOTES PER SERVING: calories 1059 | protein 42.5 g | carbohydrate 123.9 g fat 47.2 g | saturated fat 12.85 g | fibre 8.6 g | added sugar 8.8 g | salt 3.05 g

VEGETARIAN

corta spini-chilli pasta

If you like it hot, hot, hot, like I sometimes do, use a full teaspoon of chilli – if you prefer a milder flavour, simply halve that amount. Tube pasta like caserecce or rigatoni is best, as the little pockets get filled with the succulent sauce of stringy cheese.

SERVES 4 | **PREPARATION: 10 MINS | COOKING TIME: 20 MINS**

1 small aubergine, cut lengthways into 1 cm (½ in) slices
2–3 tablespoons olive oil
1 onion, chopped
2 garlic cloves, chopped
400 g (14 oz) can chopped tomatoes
1 teaspoon dried chilli flakes
350 g (12 oz) pasta shapes, such as rigatoni or caserecce
100 g (4 oz) frozen leaf spinach
100 g (4 oz) Cheddar or Gruyère, grated
salt and pepper

Pre-heat the grill to hot. Lightly brush the aubergine with oil and grill for 2–3 minutes on each side until golden brown. Meanwhile, heat 1 tablespoon of the oil in a pan and cook the onion and garlic for 3–4 minutes until golden. Stir in the tomatoes and chilli flakes, bring to the boil and simmer for 4–5 minutes. Cut the grilled aubergine slices into strips, add to the tomato sauce and cook for a further 4–5 minutes; season to taste.

Cook the pasta according to the packet instructions, adding the spinach for the last 3 minutes. Drain well and return to the pan then stir in the tomato sauce and half the cheese. Transfer to serving plates and scatter over the remaining cheese.

NUTRITION NOTES PER SERVING: calories 416 | protein 16.8 g | carbohydrate 54.9 g | fat 16 g | saturated fat 6.48 g | fibre 4.8 g | added sugar none | salt 0.83 g

You can use 200 g (7 oz) fresh spinach when it's in season: when the pasta is cooked, remove from the heat, stir in the trimmed spinach, then drain.

VEGETARIAN

yum yum nutty noodles

If you like it hot, nutty and speedy, you simply can't go wrong with this dish. Remember what they say: there's nothing like a good toss of the wok on a weekday night.

SERVES 2 | **PREPARATION: 10 MINS | COOKING TIME: 10 MINS**

1 x 85 g (3½ oz) packet vegetable-flavoured instant noodles
2 teaspoons clear honey
1 tablespoon dark soy sauce
1 tablespoon olive oil
a 2.5 cm (1 in) piece fresh root ginger, grated
2 garlic cloves, thinly sliced
2 carrots, sliced
½ red pepper and ½ yellow pepper, seeded and sliced
175 g (6 oz) very small broccoli florets
100 g (4 oz) chestnut mushrooms, thinly sliced
6 salad onions, shredded
50 g (2 oz) salted cashew nuts

Cook the noodles according to the packet instructions, then drain. Blend the honey, soy sauce and 1 tablespoon of water in a bowl and set aside.

Heat the oil in a large frying pan or wok. Add the ginger, garlic, carrots, peppers, broccoli and mushrooms and stir-fry over a high heat for 3–4 minutes until crisp but tender. Add the salad onions and stir-fry for a further 1 minute. Toss the noodles with the vegetables and sauce and heat through, then spoon onto plates. Serve sprinkled with the cashews.

NUTRITION NOTES PER SERVING: calories 511 | protein 17.8 g | carbohydrate 63.1 g
fat 22.5 g | saturated fat 0.9 g | fibre 8.3 g | added sugar 11.5 g | salt 1.36 g

To give the carrots a decorative look, cut in half lengthways, cut two thin v-shaped grooves lengthways down each half, then cut into diagonal slices.

tingling thai-spiced vegetables

Get those tastebuds tingling with this trendy Thai delight. Simply toss those veggies in a pan and stir in the heavenly sauce. I've served them on a bed of couscous, but you could use rice or pasta.

SERVES 4   PREPARATION: 10 MINS | COOKING TIME: 20 MINS

2 tablespoons vegetable oil
1 onion, sliced
650 g (1 lb 7 oz) mixed vegetables, such as carrots, broccoli, celery,
  green beans, runner beans and aubergines, chopped
2–3 teaspoons Thai red curry paste
300 ml (10 fl oz) vegetable stock
250 g (9 oz) couscous
350 ml (12 fl oz) boiling water or vegetable stock
200 ml (7 fl oz) carton coconut cream
salt and pepper
50 g (2 oz) chopped peanuts, to garnish

Heat the oil in a large pan and cook the sliced onion for 3–4 minutes until golden. If using carrots, add them before the other vegetables and fry for 2 minutes, then add the remaining vegetables and cook for a further 3 minutes. Stir in the curry paste and stock, cover and simmer for 10 minutes until the vegetables are tender but still firm.

Place the couscous in a bowl and pour over the boiling water or stock. Allow to stand for 4–5 minutes, fluffing up with a fork two or three times until the couscous becomes light and crumbly.

Stir the coconut cream into the vegetables, heat through and season. Divide the couscous between four plates, top with spicy vegetables and scatter over the chopped peanuts.

NUTRITION NOTES PER SERVING: calories 516 | protein 13 g | carbohydrate 45 g
fat 33 g | saturated fat 17 g | fibre 7 g | added sugar none | salt 0.99 g

spicy beanburgers

My beanburgers are nutritious, easy to make and taste great. The kids love to prepare them, and can't wait to eat them. If it's a nice day, why not slap 'em on the barbie?

SERVES 2 — **PREPARATION: 15 MINS | COOKING TIME: 10 MINS**

1 tablespoon vegetable oil
1 small onion, finely chopped
2 garlic cloves, finely chopped
1 small, hot, red chilli, finely chopped
100 g (4 oz) frozen chopped spinach, thawed
400 g (14 oz) can cannellini beans
50 g (2 oz) fresh white breadcrumbs
1 teaspoon ground cumin
1 tablespoon chopped fresh coriander
salt and pepper
burger buns, relish and salad, to serve

Heat the oil in a small saucepan and cook the onion, garlic and chilli for 5 minutes until softened. Squeeze the excess moisture out of the spinach and place in a large bowl.

Mash the beans well and mix with the spinach, breadcrumbs, cumin and coriander. Add the fried onion mixture and stir well together.

Season to taste and shape into four round burgers. Grill or shallow fry for a few minutes on each side until crisp and golden. Serve in burger buns with relish and salad.

NUTRITION NOTES PER SERVING: calories 302 | protein 14.5 g | carbohydrate 47 g fat 7.5 g | saturated fat 0.73 g | fibre 10.4 g | added sugar none | salt 0.94 g

VEGETARIAN

speckled-eye squash stew

This stew positively oozes goodness, yet is easy to make and tastes terrific. But the real beauty is that it's all made in one delicious pot.

SERVES 3 | PREPARATION: 15 MINS | COOKING TIME: 30 MINS

2 tablespoons olive oil
½ teaspoon cumin seeds
½ teaspoon mustard seeds
1 onion, chopped
1 garlic clove, finely chopped
1 red chilli, seeded and sliced
450 g (1 lb) potatoes, roughly chopped
2 tablespoons curry paste
600 ml (1 pint) vegetable stock
450 g (1 lb) squash (butternut, pumpkin, or kabocha), roughly diced
400 g (14 oz) can black-eyed beans, drained
2 tomatoes, each cut into six wedges
salt and pepper
2 tablespoons chopped fresh coriander or parsley, to garnish
warm naan bread and lemon wedges, to serve

Heat the olive oil in a large pan, add the seeds and cook for **1** minute; when they begin to splutter and pop add the onion, garlic and chilli and cook for **3–4** minutes until softened. Stir in the potatoes and cook for **3** minutes. Add the curry paste and vegetable stock, bring to the boil and simmer for **5** minutes. Add the squash and simmer for a further **15** minutes until the vegetables are tender. Add the black-eyed beans and tomatoes and continue to cook for **2–3** minutes; season to taste.

Divide the stew between serving plates or large shallow bowls and sprinkle over the coriander or parsley. Serve with naan bread and lemon wedges.

NUTRITION NOTES PER SERVING: calories 377 | protein 14.2 g | carbohydrate 58.1 g fat 11.4 g | saturated fat 1.3 g | fibre 10.5 g | added sugar none | salt 1.37 g

VEGETARIAN

spaghetti mount pesto

If you're lucky enough to have half a jar of sun-dried tomatoes in the fridge, toss them into the spaghetti as well to achieve a really authentic Italian flavour. To get a lovely spiral effect with the spaghetti, twirl it around a long-pronged fork then slide it onto the plate, creating a mini mountain. Ooh, your guests will be so impressed!

SERVES 4 | PREPARATION: 10 MINS | COOKING TIME: 20 MINS

350 g (12 oz) spaghetti
2 tablespoons olive oil, plus extra to serve
1 large yellow pepper, seeded and thinly sliced
1 garlic clove, sliced
1 red chilli, seeded and sliced
150 g (5 oz) peas, thawed if frozen
175 g (6 oz) chestnut mushrooms, sliced
250 g (9 oz) cherry tomatoes, halved
3 tablespoons red pesto sauce
salt and pepper
50 g (2 oz) Parmesan, shaved or grated, to serve

Cook the spaghetti in a pan of boiling salted water according to the packet instructions. Meanwhile, heat the olive oil in a frying pan, and cook the pepper for 2 minutes. Add the garlic, chilli, peas and mushrooms and stir-fry for a further 2–3 minutes until the vegetables are tender but still firm. Remove from the heat and stir in the cherry tomato halves.

Drain the spaghetti, then return to the pan. Stir in the pesto sauce and vegetables and season to taste.

To serve, spoon onto four serving plates, or twirl the pasta around a long-pronged fork and place in mounds on the plates. Scatter with Parmesan shavings, drizzle over a little oil and serve immediately.

NUTRITION NOTES PER SERVING: calories 512 | protein 21.7 g | carbohydrate 66.2 g
fat 19.8 g | saturated fat 5.22 g | fibre 11.2 g | added sugar none | salt 1.3 g

VEGETARIAN

61

mighty mexican tortilla cheesecake

Well, not cheesecake as you know it, but delightful layers of flour tortillas filled with saucy beans, vegetables and grated cheese. Go on . . . get in on the Mexican feast. A few bottles of Mexican lager help it slip down nicely.

SERVES 3 PREPARATION: 10 MINS | COOKING TIME: 25 MINS

1 tablespoon olive oil
1 onion, chopped
½-1 teaspoon hot chilli powder
400 g (14 oz) can chopped tomatoes with herbs
200 g (7 oz) frozen mixed vegetables
215 g (7¼ oz) can kidney beans, drained
5 x 25 cm (10 in) flour tortillas
150 g (5 oz) mature Cheddar, grated
salt and pepper
shredded lettuce, soured cream and chopped salad onions, to serve

---

Preheat the oven to 180°C/350°F/gas 4.

Heat the oil in a pan and cook the onion for 3–4 minutes until golden. Stir in the chilli powder and tomatoes and cook for 5 minutes, or until slightly thickened. Add the mixed vegetables and heat through for 4 minutes, or until the sauce has thickened. Stir in the beans and heat through, then season.

Place a tortilla on a heatproof plate, spread with a little of the sauce and sprinkle over a handful of cheese. Continue layering the tortillas, sauce and cheese, finishing with a sprinkling of cheese. Place the plate on a baking sheet and warm through in the hot oven for 10 minutes until the cheese has melted. Cut into wedges and serve with shredded lettuce, soured cream and salad onions.

NUTRITION NOTES PER SERVING: calories 549 | protein 25.6 g | carbohydrate 65.1 g fat 22.6 g | saturated fat 11.66 g | fibre 6.3 g | added sugar none | salt 2.42 g

VEGETARIAN

'arriba' speedy gonzales tortillas

Introduce some Mexican magic into your house by serving a stack of these tasty tortillas. If you're making a fresh guacamole, leave the avocado stone in the guacamole to prevent it from going brown – another great tip brought to you by Ainsley!

SERVES 2 | PREPARATION: 15 MINS | COOKING TIME: 5–10 MINS

1 tablespoon vegetable oil
1 onion, chopped
1 garlic clove, chopped
1 teaspoon ground cumin
400 g (14 oz) can kidney beans, drained
3 flour tortillas
100 g (4 oz) ready-made guacamole
2 tomatoes, seeded and diced
4 crisp lettuce leaves, shredded
50 g (2 oz) Red Leicester, grated
salt and pepper
coriander sprigs, to garnish (optional)

Heat the oil in a pan and cook the onion for 3–4 minutes until golden. Stir in the garlic and cumin and cook for a further 1 minute. Remove from the heat and stir in the beans. Using a potato masher, roughly crush the mixture; season to taste.

Gently heat the tortillas in a microwave or dry frying pan to make them soft and easy to roll.

Spoon the guacamole over the tortillas and scatter over the lettuce and tomatoes. Spoon the beans on top and scatter over the grated cheese. Roll up each tortilla and slice in half diagonally. Stack three halves on each serving plate and garnish with any remaining lettuce and tomato and coriander sprigs, if using.

NUTRITION NOTES PER SERVING: calories 605 | protein 23 g | carbohydrate 74 g
fat 26 g | saturated fat 7 g | fibre 14 g | added sugar none | salt 2.72 g

VEGETARIAN

guadiana tortilla olé

Tortillas taste great straight from the pan and even when cold. Leftovers are fabulous in a French-bread sandwich with a dollop of mayonnaise or tomato ketchup. And for those who like to add a touch of trivia to mealtimes, the Guadiana is a river in Spain.

SERVES 2 | **PREPARATION: 15 MINS | COOKING TIME: 30 MINS**

450 g (1 lb) new potatoes, scrubbed
2 tablespoons olive oil
1 large onion, sliced
1 large red pepper, seeded and sliced
1 garlic clove, crushed
4 eggs, beaten
2 tablespoons milk
1 tablespoon chopped fresh parsley or 1 teaspoon dried parsley
salt and pepper

Cook the potatoes in boiling water for 10–15 minutes until just tender. Drain and slice.

Meanwhile, heat the oil in a small, deep frying pan and gently cook the onion and pepper for about 5 minutes until softened and the onion is beginning to turn golden. Add the sliced potatoes and the garlic and cook for a further 5 minutes, stirring occasionally.

Beat together the eggs, milk, parsley and seasoning. Pour over the vegetables, turn the heat to the lowest setting and cook gently for about 8 minutes until the mixture is almost completely set – keep checking the underside to make sure it doesn't burn.

Use a fish slice to turn the tortilla over carefully or, if it's a little tricky, place a plate over the pan, invert the tortilla onto the plate and then slide it back into the pan. Cook for a further 2–3 minutes until the underside is golden brown. Cut into wedges and serve. Olé!

NUTRITION NOTES PER SERVING: calories 488 | protein 19.5 g | carbohydrate 52.5 g fat 23.7 g | saturated fat 4.99 g | fibre 5.6 g | added sugar none | salt 0.71 g

VEGETARIAN

fish

admired avocado salsa pasta

Talk about a feast for the eyes. This warm pasta salad is so full of colour, texture and life it will win gasps of admiration even before the first bite.

SERVES 4 | **PREPARATION: 15 MINS | COOKING TIME: 15 MINS**

350 g (12 oz) pasta bows or spirals
½ small red onion, finely chopped
1 avocado, skinned, stoned and finely diced
4 tomatoes, seeded and finely diced
2 tablespoons chopped fresh coriander
2 tablespoons fresh lime juice
3 tablespoons olive oil
2 garlic cloves, chopped
1 red chilli, seeded and thinly sliced
175 g (6 oz) fresh or canned crabmeat
salt and pepper
ground cayenne, to garnish

Cook the pasta in plenty of boiling salted water according to the packet instructions. Meanwhile, make the avocado salsa: mix together the red onion, avocado, tomatoes, coriander, lime juice and 1 tablespoon of the olive oil. Season the salsa with salt and pepper and set aside.

Heat the remaining oil in a small pan and cook the garlic and chilli for 30 seconds. Add the crabmeat to the pan and heat through briefly.

Drain the pasta and return to the pan, then stir in the warmed crabmeat mixture. Stir in half of the avocado salsa and divide between four warmed serving plates. Spoon over the remaining avocado salsa and sprinkle with a little ground cayenne pepper to garnish.

NUTRITION NOTES PER SERVING: calories 537 | protein 19 g | carbohydrate 71 g
fat 22 g | saturated fat 3 g | fibre 6 g | added sugar none | salt 0.6 g

golden tuna fish triangles

Tuna from the store-cupboard often comes to our rescue when we want a quick ingredient, and once you've tasted these you'll agree that this is one of the best ideas yet. Spice it up with a seeded, chopped green chilli.

SERVES 4 | **PREPARATION: 10 MINS | COOKING TIME: 20 MINS**

450 g (1 lb) potatoes, peeled and cubed
200 g (7 oz) can tuna in brine, drained
4 salad onions, finely chopped
2 tablespoons chopped fresh coriander or parsley
4 tablespoons soured cream
grated rind of 1 lime or ½ lemon
2 tablespoons vegetable oil
1 tablespoon plain flour
paprika, for dusting
salt and pepper
leafy green salad, cooked corn cobs, cut into thick slices,
    and sweet chilli sauce, to serve

Cook the potatoes in boiling water for 10–12 minutes. Drain and mash well then stir in the tuna, salad onions, coriander or parsley, soured cream and lime rind; season to taste. Divide into eight portions and shape into triangles.

Heat the oil in a non-stick frying pan. Dust the fish triangles with flour and cook for 3 minutes on each side until golden; drain on kitchen paper and dust lightly with paprika. Serve with salad, corn cob slices and a spoonful of sweet chilli sauce.

NUTRITION NOTES PER SERVING: calories 230 | protein 11.6 g | carbohydrate 24.6 g
fat 10.1 g | saturated fat 3.24 g | fibre 1.7 g | added sugar none | salt 0.56 g

To make a quick sweet chilli sauce, mix 4 tablespoons tomato ketchup, 1 tablespoon clear honey, ¼ teaspoon chilli powder and the juice of ½ lemon.

wicked wild fish gumbo

Gumbo is synonymous with southern American cuisine, and, just like a classic stew, everything is cooked in one pot – a real fireside meal. Although you can't be perched on a rock overlooking the Mississippi River, it's equally delicious in front of your log fire or radiator. You can use any combination of fish, but avoid oily ones like herring and mackerel.

SERVES 4 **PREPARATION: 15 MINS | COOKING TIME: 25 MINS**

2 tablespoons olive oil
1 onion, chopped
2 garlic cloves, thinly sliced
1 red chilli, seeded
   and thinly sliced
1 fennel bulb, sliced
450 g (1 lb) floury potatoes, diced
2 fresh rosemary sprigs or
   ½ teaspoon dried rosemary
150 ml (5 fl oz) dry white wine
400g (14 oz) can chopped tomatoes

1–2 tablespoons sun-dried tomato
   purée or regular tomato purée
750 ml (1¼ pints) fish stock
650 g (1 lb 7 oz) mixed fish fillets,
   such as cod, haddock and salmon,
   skinned and cut into chunks
2 tablespoons chopped fresh dill
4 tablespoons soured cream
salt and pepper
warm French bread or croutons,
   to serve

Heat the olive oil in a large pan and cook the onion for 1 minute. Add the garlic, chilli, fennel and potatoes and stir-fry for a further 3–4 minutes. Add the rosemary and wine, bring to the boil, and cook rapidly for 2 minutes. Stir in the tomatoes, purée and stock, return to the boil then simmer for 10 minutes until thickened slightly.

Add the fish and simmer gently for 4 minutes until just cooked; season to taste. Ladle into serving bowls and sprinkle with the dill; drizzle over the soured cream and serve with French bread or large, crunchy croutons.

NUTRITION NOTES PER SERVING: calories 413 | protein 34.4 g | carbohydrate 27.7 g fat 16.4 g | saturated fat 4.47 g | fibre 3.8 g | added sugar none | salt 1.47 g

This dish is delicious served with croutons. To make them, heat 3–4 tablespoons of olive oil in a frying pan. Tear half a small French stick into pieces and stir-fry until crisp and golden. Drain on kitchen paper.

fab haddie and gooey egg

This is the best double-act in town, and makes a super light and easy supper. The swirling water helps to pull the egg white together to form a well-shaped poached egg. Serve it with chunks of your favourite flavoured bread, such as olive ciabatta. Encourage your guests to break the yolk when it gets to the table – ooh, just watch it flow.

SERVES 4 | **PREPARATION: 10 MINS | COOKING TIME: 15 MINS**

1 tablespoon olive oil
1 onion, sliced
400 g (14 oz) can chopped tomatoes
2 tablespoons chopped fresh parsley, plus extra to garnish
4 x 100 g (4 oz) pieces smoked haddock, skinned
2 tablespoons white wine vinegar
4 eggs
salt and pepper
steamed broccoli, to serve

Heat the oil in a large frying pan and cook the onion for 4–5 minutes until golden. Stir in the tomatoes and parsley, and season with salt and pepper. Place the fish pieces on top, cover and simmer for about 8 minutes until the fish is cooked.

Meanwhile, add the vinegar to a medium pan of boiling water, then lower the heat slightly and swirl the water around with a spoon. Crack two of the eggs into two separate cups, then gently slide both eggs into the swirling water. Cook for 2–3 minutes until the white is set but the yolk is still runny. Remove and drain with a slotted spoon; keep warm. Repeat with the other two eggs.

Spoon the sauce and fish onto serving plates. Top each with an egg, sprinkle with parsley and season with pepper. Serve with the broccoli.

NUTRITION NOTES PER SERVING: calories 218 | protein 29 g | carbohydrate 6 g fat 9 g | saturated fat 2 g| fibre 1 g | added sugar none | salt 3.95 g

saucy salmon and leek pan pizza

Another brilliant idea that's ready in a flash. I always like a piquant sauce or topping to go with my salmon, and this little lot is a scrumptious treat. So . . . what's on TV tonight?

SERVES 4 | **PREPARATION: 15 MINS | COOKING TIME: 15 MINS**

175 g (6 oz) plain flour, plus extra
   for dusting
2 teaspoons baking powder
1 tablespoon olive oil,
   plus extra for brushing
salt and pepper

FOR THE TOPPING
1 tablespoon olive oil
2 leeks, sliced

200g (7 oz) crème fraîche
2 tomatoes, roughly chopped
215 g (7½ oz) can salmon,
   drained and flaked
100 g (4 oz) Mozzarella or
   Cheddar, grated
2 tablespoons black olives
salt and pepper
small dill sprigs, to serve

Mix together the flour, baking powder and a little salt and pepper. Make a well in the centre and mix in 100 ml (3½ fl oz) cold water to make a soft dough; knead lightly on a floured surface until smooth.

Roll the dough out to make a 28 cm (11 in) round. Brush a 30 cm (12 in) frying pan with a little oil and place over a moderate heat. Add the dough and cook for 3–4 minutes. Turn and cook the other side for a further 4–5 minutes until cooked through.

Meanwhile, make the topping: heat the olive oil in a separate frying pan and cook the leeks for 4–5 minutes until softened. Pre-heat the grill to high. Spread 5 tablespoons of the crème fraîche onto the pizza base then scatter over the leeks, tomatoes, salmon chunks, cheese and olives. Season with salt and pepper. Grill the pizza for 2–3 minutes until the cheese is golden, then spoon small dollops of crème fraîche over the top. Sprinkle with the dill sprigs and serve.

NUTRITION NOTES PER SERVING: calories 573 | protein 21.9 g | carbohydrate 40.2 g fat 37.1 g | saturated fat 17.92 g | fibre 3.2 g | added sugar none | salt 2.36 g

wan kai thai-style red curry

Thai-style curries are very 'in' at the moment. We all seem to love the combination of exotic spices with that creamy coconut taste. And to think you can have all this in about 15 minutes – it's well worth trying. The curry paste I use is available in most large supermarkets.

SERVES 4   **PREPARATION: 5 MINS | COOKING TIME: 15 MINS**

1 tablespoon sunflower oil
1 onion, thinly sliced
2 tomatoes, roughly diced
400 g (14 oz) can coconut milk
1 tablespoon Thai red curry paste
500 g (1 lb 2 oz) cubed, skinned white fish such as cod, haddock or coley
juice of ½ lemon
1 tablespoon soy sauce
a handful of fresh basil or coriander leaves
salt and pepper
cooked rice and steamed sugar-snap peas or mangetout, to serve

Heat the sunflower oil in a large, non-stick pan and cook the onion over a high heat for 4–5 minutes until beginning to brown. Add the tomatoes and cook for 1 minute then stir in the coconut milk and curry paste. Bring to a gentle simmer and add the fish; cook gently for 4–5 minutes until the fish is just tender.

Stir in the lemon juice, soy sauce and fresh herbs and season to taste. Spoon the rice into serving bowls and gently ladle over the fish curry; serve with sugar-snap peas or mangetout.

NUTRITION NOTES PER SERVING: calories 172 | protein 23.3 g | carbohydrate 9.3 g fat 4.9 g | saturated fat 0.62 g | fibre 1.7 g | added sugar none | salt 1.47 g

wicked wine-steamed mussels

I love mussels! They're cheap, quick and easy to cook yet still really sophisticated – and cooked like this they're sure to slip down a treat!

SERVES 2   **PREPARATION: 10 MINS | COOKING TIME: 10 MINS**

150 ml (5 fl oz) dry white wine
1 small onion, very finely chopped
2 garlic cloves, thinly sliced
1 red chilli, seeded and finely chopped, or a pinch of dried chilli flakes
1 kg (2¼ lb) scrubbed live mussels
a handful of fresh parsley, roughly chopped
black pepper
French bread and green salad, to serve

Pour the wine into a large saucepan with a close-fitting lid. Add the onion, garlic and chilli and bring to the boil. Simmer for 5 minutes until the onion is tender.

Meanwhile, check the mussels, discarding any that remain open when tapped sharply with a knife (if they don't close, they're dead and should not be eaten). Add the mussels to the pan with a good grinding of black pepper. Cover and steam for 3–5 minutes, shaking the pan occasionally, until all the shells have just opened. Discard any that do not open after cooking.

Sprinkle the parsley over and ladle the mussels and the wine juices into large bowls and serve with plenty of bread and salad.

NUTRITION NOTES PER SERVING: calories 178 | protein 19.8 g | carbohydrate 5.5 g
fat 3.3 g | saturated fat 0.55 g | fibre 1.7 g | added sugar none | salt 1.13 g

Mussels, which you can buy from autumn through to spring, are naturally quite salty, so don't go mad on the seasoning.

tossed beansprout prawn noodle

When we buy prawns in this country they are generally frozen. You can get small pink ones up to large tiger prawns, which can be a lot more expensive, but are truly worth it for that special occasion. So, if you're feeling a bit flash, use tiger prawns, but if you're feeling unoysterish, use another type of mushroom.

SERVES 2 | PREPARATION: 10 MINS | COOKING TIME: 5 MINS

175g (6 oz) medium egg noodles
2 tablespoons vegetable oil
1 garlic clove, chopped, or 1 teaspoon garlic purée
1 tablespoon chopped fresh coriander or parsley
6 salad onions, diagonally sliced
1 red chilli, seeded and chopped
100g (4 oz) mushrooms, such as oyster, chestnut or button, sliced
100g (4 oz) large cooked, peeled prawns
3 tablespoons oyster sauce
1 tablespoon fresh lime juice
2 teaspoons caster sugar
100 g (4 oz) fresh beansprouts
coriander or parsley sprigs, to garnish

Cook the noodles for 4 minutes, or according to the packet instructions, then drain well.

Meanwhile, heat the vegetable oil in a frying pan and stir-fry the garlic, coriander or parsley, salad onion slices and chilli for 1 minute. Add the mushrooms and prawns and stir-fry for a further 1 minute.

Stir in 120 ml (4 fl oz) water, the oyster sauce, lime juice and sugar; cook briefly to heat through and reduce slightly. Stir in the noodles and beansprouts and heat through. Garnish with a sprinkling of coriander or parsley, toss and serve. May I recommend chop sticks?

NUTRITION NOTES PER SERVING: calories 560 | protein 29 g | carbohydrate 70 g fat 20 g | saturated fat 2 g | fibre 2 g | added sugar trace | salt 5.32 g

simply smokin' paella

And no, I don't mean put it in a pipe or set it alight. I'm talking about smoked ham, which gives this easy-peasy paella a distinctive flavour. Another dish that's cooked in one pot – that'll save on the washing up.

SERVES 4 | **PREPARATION: 10 MINS | COOKING TIME: 25 MINS**

2 tablespoons vegetable oil
1 onion, sliced
1 red pepper, seeded and diced
1 garlic clove, crushed
200 g (7 oz) long-grain rice
175 g (6 oz) smoked ham, roughly diced
900 ml (1½ pints) chicken or vegetable stock
½ teaspoon each paprika and turmeric
175 g (6 oz) large prawns, thawed if frozen
100 g (4 oz) frozen peas
salt and pepper

Heat the oil in a large frying pan and cook the onion for 3–4 minutes until softened and golden. Add the red pepper, garlic and rice and stir-fry for 1 minute. Add the ham, stock, paprika and turmeric, bring to the boil and simmer for 12 minutes.

Stir in the prawns and peas and cook for a further 3–4 minutes until the rice and vegetables are tender. Season to taste, then divide between four serving plates and serve immediately. Ooh, how about a glass of Rioja?

NUTRITION NOTES PER SERVING: calories 380 | protein 25 g | carbohydrate 52 g fat 10 g | saturated fat 2 g | fibre 3 g | added sugar none | salt 4.12 g

Saffron is the traditional method for giving paella its yellow colour, but it is expensive. If you do have some, replace the turmeric and paprika with a large pinch of saffron threads.

cod kebabs with aztec salsa

This dish presents beautifully, and is ideal for a quick supper. My lively lime marinade really firms up the fish nicely for grilling. To add an extra kick to your salsa, simply add one small, fresh, seeded, chopped chilli.

SERVES 3   PREPARATION: 15 MINS | COOKING TIME: 15 MINS

450 g (1lb) skinned thick
   cod fillets, cubed
grated rind of 1 lime
juice of 2 limes
3 tablespoons olive oil
3 tomatoes, seeded and chopped
1 small red onion, finely chopped

1 tablespoon chopped fresh
   parsley or coriander
1 tablespoon drained capers
1 courgette, diagonally sliced
225 g (8 oz) tagliatelle
salt and pepper

Mix together the cubed cod, lime rind, half the lime juice and 1 tablespoon of the oil. Season with salt and pepper and set aside to marinate for 5 minutes.

Mix the tomato flesh, onion, 1 tablespoon of the oil, the parsley or coriander, capers and the remaining lime juice.

Preheat the grill to high. Thread the cod cubes and courgette slices on to six bamboo skewers, season and grill for 8–10 minutes, turning once, until tender and golden.

Meanwhile, cook the tagliatelle in a large pan of boiling, salted water, according to packet instructions. Drain, then toss with the remaining oil. Fork some tagliatelle into the centre of each plate, top with two kebabs and spoon over some salsa.

NUTRITION NOTES PER SERVING: calories 504 | protein 37 g | carbohydrate 61 g fat 14 g | saturated fat 2 g | fibre 4 g | added sugar none | salt 0.74 g

If using wooden or bamboo skewers, first soak them in warm water for 10 minutes to prevent them burning.

crunch lunch
cod and mash

You can buy all manner of smoked fish: trout, eel, mackerel, salmon, cod and kippers (known as herrings before they get kippered), to name but a few. Remember to look for nice moist flesh when buying. This snappy dish is ready to serve in a flash.

SERVES 4 | **PREPARATION: 15 MINS | COOKING TIME: 15 MINS**

15 g (½ oz) butter, plus extra for greasing
4 x 150 g (5 oz) smoked cod fillets, skinned
6 salad onions
4 tomatoes, sliced
8 black olives, pitted and chopped
2 tablespoons olive oil
3 tablespoons torn fresh basil leaves
25 g (1 oz) fresh white breadcrumbs
700 g (1 lb 9 oz) potatoes, chopped
4–5 tablespoons milk
salt and pepper

Preheat the oven to 200°C/400°F/gas 6.

Place the fish in a buttered ovenproof dish and season. Chop the white parts from the onions, slice and scatter over the cod. Arrange the tomatoes on top of the fish and scatter over the olives. Drizzle over half the oil and sprinkle with half the basil. Toss the breadcrumbs with the remaining basil, season, and scatter over the fish. Drizzle over the remaining oil and bake for 15 minutes until the fish is cooked.

Meanwhile, cook the potatoes in a pan of boiling, salted water for 10–15 minutes. Drain well then add the milk and mash to a soft consistency. Push the mash to one side of the pan, add the butter and heat. Finely chop the green parts of the onions, add to the pan and fry briefly. Stir the onions into the mash; season.

Divide the onion mash between four serving plates and place the cod on top. Spoon around the fish juices and serve.

NUTRITION NOTES PER SERVING: calories 384 | protein 33 g | carbohydrate 39 g
fat 12 g | saturated fat 3 g | fibre 4 g | added sugar none | salt 5.32 g

FISH

chilli-lemon-splashed fish

It's fluffy, it's puffy, it's pulling in the crowds. I am, of course, referring to couscous. It's a great store-cupboard standby as it's pre-cooked and is ready to serve in just a couple of minutes. Go on, give it a try – it'll give mealtimes a fluffy feel.

SERVES 4 | **PREPARATION: 15 MINS | COOKING TIME: 15 MINS**

1 lemon
4 x 120 g (4½ oz) cod or
   haddock fillets, unskinned
3 tablespoons olive oil,
   plus extra for brushing
2 garlic cloves, finely chopped
1 red pepper, seeded
   and finely diced
175 g (6 oz) couscous

300 ml (10 fl oz) hot
   vegetable stock
2 tomatoes, finely diced
4 salad onions, finely chopped
2 tablespoons chopped
   fresh coriander or parsley
¼ teaspoon chilli powder
salt and pepper

Pre-heat the grill to high.

Cut four slices from the lemon and squeeze the juice from the remainder into a small bowl. Place the fish fillets on the grill pan, skin-side up, and lay the lemon slices on top; brush with a little olive oil and season with salt and pepper. Grill for 6–8 minutes, without turning, until cooked and golden.

Meanwhile, heat 1 tablespoon of the olive oil in a large pan and cook the garlic and pepper for 4–5 minutes until softened. Stir in the couscous, hot stock, tomatoes, salad onions and coriander or parsley. Season to taste, cover and remove from the heat.

Mix the lemon juice with the remaining 2 tablespoons of oil and the chilli powder. Fork up the couscous until fluffy then spoon onto serving plates, place the fish on top and drizzle over the chilli dressing.

NUTRITION NOTES PER SERVING: calories 302 | protein 25.8 g | carbohydrate 28.2 g fat 10.1 g | saturated fat 1.42 g | fibre 1.2 g | added sugar none | salt 0.77 g

citrus-crusted cod with cajun spuds

An impressive meal that's full of colour, texture and taste. Try with other types of fish like haddock, salmon, pollock, bream or sea bass.

SERVES 4 | **PREPARATION: 10 MINS | COOKING TIME: 20 MINS**

4 x 150 g (5 oz) red-skinned potatoes, cooked and cut into six wedges
3 tablespoons olive oil, plus extra for brushing
1 teaspoon Cajun seasoning or paprika
4 x 150 g (5 oz) cod fillets, skinned
2 tablespoons sun-dried tomato paste
40 g (1½ oz) fresh white breadcrumbs
1 tablespoon chopped fresh parsley
grated rind and juice of 1 lemon
4 tomatoes, seeded and finely chopped
4 salad onions, finely chopped
salt and pepper
steamed broccoli, to serve

Pre-heat the oven to 220°C/450°F/gas 7. Arrange the potato wedges on a baking sheet, lightly brush with oil and sprinkle with Cajun seasoning and a little salt. Roast for 12–15 minutes until golden brown.

Meanwhile, season the cod fillets and spread each with the sun-dried tomato paste. Mix together the breadcrumbs, parsley, lemon rind, a splash of lemon juice and some seasoning. Press the crumb mixture on top of the paste-covered fish to make a crust.

Heat 1 tablespoon of the olive oil in a non-stick frying pan. Cook the fish, crust-side down, for 2–3 minutes until golden. Place in an ovenproof dish, crust-side up, and bake for 8–10 minutes until cooked.

To make the salsa, mix the tomatoes, salad onions, remaining oil and lemon juice in a bowl and season to taste. Serve the fish with the potato wedges, tomato salsa and steamed broccoli.

NUTRITION NOTES PER SERVING: calories 360 | protein 31.1 g | carbohydrate 36.6 g fat 10.9 g | saturated fat 1.5 g | fibre 2.9 g | added sugar none | salt 1.07 g

rocky road potato cod

A mid-week meal that's good for the holidays. Make the pie ahead if you like, chill, then cook for slightly longer. Try to use King Edward or Maris Piper potatoes.

SERVES 4 | **PREPARATION: 15 MINS | COOKING TIME: 45 MINS**

900 g (2 lb) potatoes, cubed
450 g (1 lb) cod fillet, skinned
  and cut into large chunks
175 g (6 oz) peeled prawns
1 tablespoon vegetable oil
1 onion, chopped
6 rashers streaky bacon, chopped
150 g (5 oz) button mushrooms

200 g (7 oz) soft cheese
150 ml (5 fl oz) single cream
4 tablespoons chopped
  fresh parsley
grated rind of 1 lemon
salt and pepper
steamed green vegetables such as
  broccoli and mangetout, to serve

Preheat the oven to 190°C/375°F/gas 5. Cook the potatoes in a large pan of boiling salted water for 8–10 minutes until almost tender.

Meanwhile, arrange the cod evenly in the base of a 1.5 litre (2½ pint) pie dish and scatter over the prawns. Heat the oil in a pan and cook the onion and bacon for 5 minutes. Add the mushrooms and cook for a further minute. Spoon over the fish.

Warm the soft cheese in the same pan until melted then stir in the cream and half the parsley. Season to taste and pour over the fish. Roughly spoon over the potatoes and sprinkle with the lemon rind and remaining parsley. Season with salt and pepper and bake for 20–25 minutes until the fish is cooked. Place under the grill, pre-heated to medium, for 5 minutes until the top is nicely browned.

NUTRITION NOTES PER SERVING: calories 720 | protein 44.1 g | carbohydrate 43.4 g
fat 42.2 g | saturated fat 10.95 g | fibre 4.3 g | added sugar none | salt 2.62 g

garlic butter sole with citrus mash

Lemon sole is a super fish with a mild flavour. It is best cooked quickly so it doesn't dry out and retains that subtle flavour. Your fishmonger will fillet the whole sole for you – all you need to do is ask. If you're feeling posh, use Dover sole instead.

SERVES 2   PREPARATION: 10 MINS | COOKING TIME: 15 MINS

450 g (1 lb) floury potatoes, cubed
a knob of butter, at room temperature
1 garlic clove, crushed
2 tablespoons chopped fresh parsley
2 x 120 g (4½ oz) lemon sole fillets, unskinned
150 ml (5 fl oz) double cream
grated rind and juice of 1 lemon
salt and black pepper
steamed vegetables such as mangetout and spinach, to serve

Cook the potatoes in a large pan of boiling, salted water for 10–12 minutes until tender.

Pre-heat the grill to high. Meanwhile, mix together the butter, garlic, parsley, a little salt and plenty of black pepper. Cook the sole skin-side up under the grill for 1–2 minutes. Turn over the fish, dot with the herbed butter and return to the grill for a further 2–3 minutes until golden and cooked through.

Meanwhile, heat the cream and lemon rind in a small pan. Drain the potatoes and mash well, then beat in the warm, zesty cream until smooth and fluffy. Season well to taste, then spoon on to serving plates. Arrange the sole fillets on top of the mash and drizzle over a little of the fresh lemon juice. Serve with steamed green vegetables.

NUTRITION NOTES PER SERVING: calories 650 | protein 27.7 g | carbohydrate 41.8 g fat 42.4 g | saturated fat 25.77 g | fibre 3.5 g | added sugar none | salt 0.76 g

Let those juices flow. Ooh... what am I like?

cawley's classic fish and chips

You can't beat fish and chips and the key to their success is a crispy batter. The brilliant batter in this dish comes courtesy of my mate Richard Cawley who served up a winner on *Ready Steady Cook*.

SERVES 2 | PREPARATION: 10 MINS | COOKING TIME: 20 MINS

2 large floury potatoes
2 x 175 g (6 oz) cod fillets,
    unskinned
sunflower oil, for deep frying
tartare sauce and lemon wedges,
    to serve

FOR THE BATTER
4 tablespoons plain flour, plus
    extra for dusting
1 teaspoon bicarbonate of soda
100 ml (3½ fl oz) cold water
juice of 1 lemon
salt and pepper

Scrub the potatoes in clean, cold water and cut into fingers as thick or thin as you like. Wash well, rinsing off excess starch to stop them sticking together, and dry thoroughly with kitchen paper. Heat the sunflower oil in a deep frying pan until the oil is hot enough for a cube of bread to turn brown in about 1 minute. Cook the chips for 5–7 minutes or until pale golden. Remove with a slotted spoon and drain on kitchen paper. Dust the cod in a little flour, shaking off any excess.

Make the batter: place the flour and bicarbonate of soda in a bowl and whisk in the water to make a smooth batter. Stir in the lemon juice and a pinch of salt. Dip the dusted cod into the batter, shaking off any excess, and deep fry in the hot oil for 5 minutes until the batter is deep golden and the fish is cooked through. Drain on kitchen paper and keep warm. Raise the heat slightly and when the oil is hot enough to brown a cube of bread in 30 seconds, return the chips to the pan for 1–2 minutes until crisp. Drain on kitchen paper and sprinkle with salt. Serve the crispy fish and chips with a good spoonful of tartare sauce and lemon wedges for squeezing over.

NUTRITION NOTES PER SERVING: calories 712 | protein 38.1 g | carbohydrate 64.7 g fat 35.1 g | saturated fat 4.62 g | fibre 3.7 g | added sugar none | salt 1.32 g

It's easy to make your own tartare sauce – just stir together some mayonnaise with a few chopped gherkins, capers, onion and parsley.

a spicy poultry spin on tradition

jimmy's chicken kiev

Chicken Kiev is one of those old favourites that everyone loves, especially my kids. My butter bean purée brings it back into the nineties with a bang!

SERVES 2 | **PREPARATION: 15 MINS | COOKING TIME: 15 MINS**

2 x 75 g (3 oz) boneless, skinless
chicken breasts
40 g (1½ oz) unsalted butter,
at room temperature
4 tablespoons chopped
fresh parsley
2 garlic cloves, crushed
50 g (2 oz) fresh white
breadcrumbs
1 tablespoon freshly
grated Parmesan
1 tablespoon plain flour,
seasoned with salt and pepper
1 egg, beaten
1-2 tablespoons vegetable oil

FOR THE BUTTER BEAN PURÉE

1 tablespoon olive oil
1 small onion, finely chopped
400 g (14 oz) can butter beans,
drained
75 g (3 oz) mature Cheddar
or Gruyère, finely diced
a knob of butter
2 tablespoons chopped
fresh coriander (optional)
a few drops Tabasco
or other hot chilli sauce
salt and pepper
lemon wedges and green salad,
to serve

Using a small knife, horizontally cut a pocket into each chicken breast. Mix together the butter, parsley, garlic and plenty of salt and pepper. Spoon the mixture into the pocket of each chicken breast. Stir together the breadcrumbs and Parmesan. Dust the chicken breasts in the seasoned flour then the beaten egg and finally, roll in the breadcrumb mixture. Heat the vegetable oil in a large frying pan and cook the chicken for 5-6 minutes on each side until golden brown and cooked through.

To make the butter bean purée heat the olive oil in a small pan and cook the onion for 5 minutes until softened. Add the beans to the pan and cook gently for 2-3 minutes, stirring occasionally, until warmed through. Add the cheese to the pan with the butter, stirring until melted. Using a hand blender, whizz the mixture until smooth and creamy. Stir in the coriander, if using, and add salt, pepper and Tabasco to taste. Spoon the purée onto serving plates and top with the chicken Kiev. Serve with lemon wedges and crisp green salad.

NUTRITION NOTES PER SERVING: calories 863 | protein 45.3 g | carbohydrate 55.8 g fat 52.5 g | saturated fat 25.07 g | fibre 9.5 g | added sugar none | salt 2 g

mozzarella-oozing rosemary chicken

This is based on a Neapolitan dish. Lots of people think that rosemary was made for lamb, but it goes equally well with chicken. In fact, I think this will get you the 'ooh!' approval. Use fresh rosemary if you like, making the quantity up to two teaspoons of the chopped herb.

SERVES 4 | **PREPARATION: 10 MINS | COOKING TIME: 20 MINS**

150 g (5 oz) Mozzarella, drained
1½ teaspoons dried rosemary
¼ teaspoon dried chilli flakes
8 boneless chicken thighs
1 tablespoon plain flour
olive oil, for brushing

700 g (1lb 9 oz) potatoes, cubed
25 g (1 oz) butter
1 leek, cut into 6 mm (¼ in) coins
2 tablespoons milk or single cream
salt and pepper

Pre-heat the grill to high. Cut the Mozzarella in half widthways, then cut each half into four wedges. Mix the rosemary and chilli with salt and pepper in a bowl, then toss the cheese in it.

Lay the chicken out flat, sprinkle with the flour and place a cheese wedge in the centre of each. Roll the chicken round the cheese and secure with wooden cocktail sticks, tucking in the ends, if possible. Place in a roasting tin, brush with oil, season and grill for 20 minutes, turning occasionally, until cooked through.

Meanwhile, cook the potatoes in a pan of boiling, salted water for 10–15 minutes until tender; drain well and keep warm. Melt the butter in a frying pan and stir-fry the leek for 3–4 minutes until softened. Mash the potatoes with the milk or cream, then stir in the leeks and season to taste. Divide the leek mash between four serving plates, remove the cocktail sticks from the chicken and place on top; spoon round the chicken-pan juices and serve.

NUTRITION NOTES PER SERVING: calories 605 | protein 35 g | carbohydrate 36 g
fat 36 g | saturated fat 15 g | fibre 3 g | added sugar none | salt 1.21 g

turkey dumplings with spicy broth

Okay, it is a bit unusual to see an English-style meatball made with these Oriental flavourings, but trust me, it's fabulous! I have even been known to crumble a few prawn crackers on top just before serving.

SERVES 2 | **PREPARATION: 10 MINS | COOKING TIME: 15 MINS**

175 g (6 oz) minced turkey
3 salad onions, finely chopped
2 tablespoons chopped
   fresh coriander
1 tablespoon dry sherry
1 tablespoon cornflour
½ teaspoon Chinese
   five-spice powder
pinch salt
2 salad onions, thinly sliced, and
   2 teaspoons toasted sesame
   seeds, to serve

FOR THE BROTH
300 ml (10 fl oz) hot chicken stock
2 teaspoons Thai red curry paste
2 teaspoons soy sauce
200 g (7 fl oz) carton
   coconut cream
4 leaves Cos lettuce, shredded
juice of ½ lime
salt and pepper

Place the turkey, chopped salad onions, coriander, sherry, cornflour, five-spice powder and salt in a bowl and mix well together. Shape the mixture into **12** small balls.

To make the broth, place the stock, curry paste and soy sauce in a large pan and gently bring to the boil. Season to taste then add the dumplings and simmer gently for **8–10** minutes until the dumplings are cooked. Stir in the coconut cream, lettuce leaves and lime juice and heat gently for **1** minute.

Ladle the broth into serving bowls and sprinkle over the salad onions and toasted sesame seeds.

NUTRITION NOTES PER SERVING: calories 517 | protein 25.3 g | carbohydrate 17.1 g fat 38.2 g | saturated fat 30.46 g | fibre 1.6 g | added sugar 0.1 g | salt 1.81 g

lightning coq au vin

We all like a bit of coq au vin once in a while, and mine is well worth remembering, especially as it's ready to eat in lightning time, which is great as, traditionally, this dish is cooked over a long period. Go on, get your coq au vin in.

SERVES 4   PREPARATION: 15 MINS | COOKING TIME: 25 MINS

750 g (1 lb 10 oz) floury
  potatoes, diced
4–5 tablespoons olive oil
6 boneless, skinless chicken
  thighs, halved
1 tablespoon flour,
  seasoned with salt and pepper
8 button onions, quartered
4 rashers smoked streaky bacon,
  cut into strips
100 g (4 oz) button
  mushrooms, quartered

1 garlic clove, crushed
2 tablespoons brandy
300 ml (10 fl oz) red wine
2 fresh thyme sprigs or
  ½ teaspoon dried thyme
1 tablespoon tomato purée
2 teaspoons cornflour
2 tablespoons chopped fresh parsley
salt and pepper

Cook the diced potatoes in a large pan of boiling, salted water for 10–15 minutes until tender. Meanwhile, heat 1 tablespoon of the oil in a large pan. Dust the chicken thighs with seasoned flour and cook in the pan for 1–2 minutes on each side. Add the onions and bacon and cook for 2–3 minutes, then add the mushrooms and garlic and stir-fry for a further 2 minutes until well browned. Pour over the brandy and carefully ignite.

When the flames have subsided, pour in the red wine and bring to the boil. Add the thyme and tomato purée and simmer gently for 15 minutes until the chicken is cooked. Mix the cornflour to a smooth paste with a little water and stir it in, return to the boil and cook for a minute or so, stirring until thickened; season to taste.

Drain the potatoes and mash well. Stir in the remaining olive oil and the parsley; season to taste. Divide among the serving plates and spoon over the coq au vin. Serve immediately.

NUTRITION NOTES PER SERVING: calories 592 | protein 29.4 g | carbohydrate 42.8 g fat 27.4 g | saturated fat 7.44 g | fibre 3.7 g | added sugar none | salt 1.52 g

zesty chick fric

This is just like that old classic, fricassee, and by having the chicken boned you'll save bags of time. Using thighs keeps the meat juicy, just the way I like it. Why not use the egg whites to make a quick dessert (see page 180)?

SERVES 2 | **PREPARATION: 15 MINS | COOKING TIME: 30 MINS**

4 boneless chicken thighs
120 g (4½ oz) pack boil-in-the-bag
  basmati rice
2 tablespoons olive oil
1 large onion, thinly sliced
1 carrot, diced
1 celery stick, roughly diced
1 garlic clove, finely chopped
1 tablespoon plain flour

300 ml (10 fl oz) hot chicken stock
grated rind and juice of 1 lemon
50 g (2 oz) frozen peas
3 egg yolks
2 tablespoons chopped fresh
  parsley
salt and pepper
quartered lemon slices, to garnish

Pre-heat the oven to 220°C/425°F/gas 7. Heat a heavy-based frying pan. Cut each chicken thigh into 4 pieces and place skin-side down in the frying pan. Cook for 8–10 minutes, turning once, until crisp and golden brown. Cook the rice according to packet instructions.

Heat the olive oil in a large sauté pan or a frying pan with a lid and cook the onion, carrot, celery and garlic for 3–4 minutes, stirring until golden. Add the flour to the vegetables, stirring with a wooden spoon, and cook for 1 minute before gradually adding the stock and lemon rind; bring to the boil then simmer for 3–4 minutes.

Add the chicken to the pan of saucy vegetables, cover and simmer for 3 minutes until the vegetables are tender.

Stir the peas and plenty of salt and pepper into the chicken mixture and cook for 1–2 minutes. Beat the egg yolks, then stir in the lemon juice. Over a gentle heat add the egg yolk mixture to the chicken and stir for a few minutes to thicken the sauce, then stir in the parsley; season to taste.

Spoon the chicken mixture onto a serving plate, garnish with lemon slices, and serve with the rice.

NUTRITION NOTES PER SERVING: calories 862 | protein 40.6 g | carbohydrate 73.4 g
fat 47.1 g | saturated fat 11.91 g | fibre 4.9 g | added sugar none | salt 1.11 g

liver and bacon with tsar mash

Some things we like, some things we're not too sure about. Well . . . if you like chicken livers this recipe will be used again and again and if you're not sure, it's bound to win you over. A real explosive taste that leaves the dishes satisfyingly clean. Buy the chicken livers from your butcher, or check out the freezer section in your supermarket.

SERVES 2 | **PREPARATION: 5 MINS | COOKING TIME: 10 MINS**

500 g (1 lb 2 oz) potatoes, peeled and diced
1 tablespoon olive oil
4 rashers streaky bacon
200 g (7 oz) trimmed chicken livers
1 tablespoon red wine vinegar
2 tablespoons port
150 g (5 oz) carton soured cream
salt and freshly ground black pepper
snipped chives, to garnish

Cook the potatoes in a large pan of boiling, salted water for 8–10 minutes until tender. Heat the oil in a large frying pan and cook the bacon for 1 minute. Add the chicken livers and cook over a high heat for 1–2 minutes on each side until well browned but still pink in the centre; season to taste. Transfer to a heatproof dish and place in the bottom of the oven to keep warm.

Pour the vinegar and port into the hot pan and bubble vigorously for 1 minute. Stir in half the soured cream, lower the heat and simmer gently for 2–3 minutes until thickened.

Drain the potatoes and return to the pan. Mash well then beat in the remaining soured cream, season to taste.

Pile the mash onto two serving plates and spoon the liver and bacon on top. Season the soured cream sauce and drizzle over. Garnish with snipped chives and coarsely ground black pepper and serve immediately.

NUTRITION NOTES PER SERVING: calories 756 | protein 33.9 g | carbohydrate 48.3 g fat 47 g | saturated fat 19.99 g | fibre 3.3 g | added sugar 1.8 g | salt 2.5 g

clever cook's roast chicken dinner

We all have to be pretty crafty in the kitchen at times, and this speedy dinner of roast chicken, honeyed potatoes, bacon-wrapped sausages, stir-fried broccoli and bread sauce has got me out of hot water on more than one occasion. Y'know that lunch invitation you booked weeks ago but forgot about until the unexpected Sunday 12pm phonecall – 'We're on our way'? Help!

SERVES 2 | PREPARATION: 15 MINS | COOKING TIME 25 MINS

4 x 100 g (4 oz) potatoes,
   each halved lengthways
2 x 100 g (4 oz) boneless
   chicken breasts
a large knob of butter
2 rashers smoked streaky bacon
4 chipolata sausages
1 small onion, finely chopped
150 ml (5 fl oz) milk

40 g (1½ oz) fresh
   white breadcrumbs
a pinch of ground nutmeg
1 tablespoon clear honey
2 tablespoons olive oil
1 garlic clove, thinly sliced
200 g (7 oz) broccoli florets
salt and pepper

Preheat the oven to 220°C/450°F/gas 7. Cook the potatoes in a large pan of boiling, salted water for 10–15 minutes until just tender. Meanwhile, place the chicken breasts in a roasting tin, season well and dot with a little butter. Roast in the oven for 25 minutes until golden brown and cooked through. Meanwhile, stretch the bacon with the back of a knife and cut each rasher in half widthways. Wrap a half rasher around each chipolata and add to the chicken pan.

Heat the remaining butter in a small pan and cook the onion for 3–4 minutes until softened, then pour in the milk and bring to the boil. Lower the heat, stir in the breadcrumbs and nutmeg; season to taste and keep warm.

Drain the potatoes and return to the pan. Toss with the honey and one tablespoon of the oil and arrange around the chicken in the roasting tin. Return to the oven for 8–10 minutes until golden brown. Heat the remaining oil in a wok and stir-fry the garlic and broccoli for 2 minutes. Add a splash of water and cook for a further 2 minutes until tender. Season to taste. Place the chicken breasts on large serving plates with the honeyed potatoes, bacon-wrapped sausages, stir-fried broccoli and bread sauce.

NUTRITION NOTES PER SERVING: calories 919 | protein 45.5 g | carbohydrate 73.8 g fat 51 g | saturated fat 17.91 g | fibre 6.5 g | added sugar 9.6 g | salt 3.11 g

acapulco chicken

An idea created from lots of left-over broken tortilla chips and now a family favourite. Even friends request it when coming over for a casual supper. One teaspoon of chilli if you like it hot, two if you like it hot, hot, hot. Can you feel it?

SERVES 4   **PREPARATION: 10 MINS | COOKING TIME: 30 MINS**

1 tablespoon vegetable oil
8 boneless, skinless chicken thighs, cut into chunks
1 onion, sliced
2 garlic cloves, chopped
1–2 teaspoons chilli powder, plus extra for sprinkling
400 g (14 oz) can chopped tomatoes
175 ml (6 fl oz) chicken stock
400 g (14 oz) can kidney beans, drained
½ teaspoon dried oregano
100 g (4 oz) tortilla chips
salt and pepper
soured cream and parsley sprigs, to garnish
cooked rice, to serve

Heat the oil in a pan, add the chicken, onion and garlic and cook for about 5 minutes until golden. Add the chilli and stir-fry for 30 seconds, then add the tomatoes, stock, kidney beans and oregano; season with salt and pepper, bring to the boil, cover and simmer for 20 minutes or until the chicken is tender.

Transfer the chicken to a serving dish and sprinkle over the tortilla chips. Top with a dollop of soured cream, some parsley sprigs and a sprinkling of chilli powder. Serve with rice.

NUTRITION NOTES PER SERVING: calories 596 | protein 31 g | carbohydrate 52 g fat 31 g | saturated fat 7 g | fibre 7 g | added sugar none | salt 1.95 g

cha-cha-cha chimichangas

Chimichangas are simply fried Mexican tortillas. That'll get you cha-cha-cha-ing around your kitchen.

SERVES 4   **PREPARATION: 15 MINS | COOKING TIME: 15 MINS**

sunflower oil, for frying
1 onion, finely chopped
1 red pepper, seeded and diced
2 boneless, skinless chicken thighs, roughly chopped
2 green chillies, seeded and thinly sliced
2 garlic cloves, finely chopped
2 tomatoes, roughly chopped
100 g (4 oz) frozen sweetcorn, thawed
4 tablespoons taco sauce
4 salad onions, finely chopped
4 large flour tortillas
shredded lettuce, soured cream and ready-made guacamole, to serve

Heat the sunflower oil in a large pan and stir-fry the onion, pepper and chicken thighs over a high heat for 3–4 minutes until well browned. Stir in the chillies, garlic, tomatoes and sweetcorn and cook for a further 2–3 minutes until the chicken is cooked through.

Stir in the taco sauce and salad onions and set aside to cool a little.

Warm one of the tortillas in a hot, dry frying pan until soft and flexible. Spoon a quarter of the cooled chicken mixture into the centre of the tortilla and fold over the edges to form a neat parcel; pin in place with cocktail sticks and repeat with the remaining tortillas.

Heat 1 cm (½ in) vegetable oil in a large frying pan and cook the chimichangas for 2–3 minutes on each side until crisp and golden brown. Drain on kitchen paper and serve hot with shredded lettuce, soured cream and guacamole.

NUTRITION NOTES PER SERVING: calories 374 | protein 12.8 g | carbohydrate 38.2 g fat 19.9 g | saturated fat 3.01 g | fibre 3.1 g | added sugar none | salt 0.42 g

sos chicken with pilau rice

'S' for succulent, 'O' for orgasmic, 'S' for saucy; and all this in just 15 minutes. Ooh, you lucky people.

SERVES 4	PREPARATION: 5 MINS | COOKING TIME: 10 MINS

500 g (1 lb 2 oz) carton
  creamed tomatoes
1–2 tablespoons hot curry paste
500 g (1 lb 2 oz) cooked boneless
  tandoori or tikka chicken breasts
  or thighs, cut into bite-sized pieces
150 ml (5 fl oz) double cream
½ teaspoon caster sugar
salt and pepper

FOR THE RICE
1 tablespoon vegetable oil
1 onion, sliced
25 g (1 oz) flaked almonds
500 g (1 lb 2 oz) cooked white rice
1 teaspoon ground turmeric
25 g (1 oz) seedless raisins
salt and pepper
chopped fresh coriander,
  to garnish (optional)

Place the creamed tomatoes in a small pan, stir in the curry paste and heat gently.

Meanwhile, for the rice, heat the oil in a wok and stir-fry the onion for 2 minutes, add the almonds and cook for a further 2 minutes until both are nicely browned. Stir in the rice, turmeric and raisins and heat gently for 3–4 minutes, adding a splash of water if the mixture is a little dry.

Add the chicken and cream to the tomato mixture, bring to the boil and simmer for 2 minutes until warmed through. Stir in the sugar and season to taste.

Season the rice and divide between serving plates. Spoon over the butter chicken and garnish with coriander, if using.

NUTRITION NOTES PER SERVING: calories 687 | protein 44.5 g | carbohydrate 55.8 g fat 33.2 g | saturated fat 14.13 g | fibre 2.8 g | added sugar 4.4 g | salt 1.3 g

I make this using left-over rice, but cooked rice is now available in free-flow frozen form or in cans.

gorgeous chicken korma

My chicken korma is based on a spicy, creamy dish from Kashmir. It's incredibly easy to make and very, very tasty. Chicken korma is popular because the flavours blend together perfectly, leaving that gorgeous taste lingering on your tastebuds 'til the next mouthful.

SERVES 4 | **PREPARATION: 10 MINS | COOKING TIME: 30 MINS**

1 tablespoon vegetable oil
1 onion, roughly chopped
350 ml (12 fl oz) natural yogurt
200 ml (7 fl oz) double cream
25 g (1 oz) butter
½ teaspoon salt
1 teaspoon ground turmeric
2 teaspoons hot chilli powder
3 garlic cloves, crushed

3 tablespoons ground almonds
4 x 100 g (4 oz) boneless,
 skinless chicken breasts, each
 cut into six pieces
toasted flaked almonds and
 coriander sprigs,
 to garnish (optional)
naan bread or rice, and cucumber
 and red onion salad, to serve

Pre-heat the oven to 200°C/400°F/gas 6.

Heat the oil in a small pan and cook the onion for 5 minutes until softened. Place in a food processor with the yogurt, cream, butter, salt, turmeric, chilli, garlic and almonds and whizz until well blended.

Arrange the chicken in a greased casserole dish and pour over the korma mixture. Bake for 30 minutes until the chicken is cooked through. Spoon onto plates, garnish with flaked almonds and coriander sprigs, if you wish, and serve with naan or rice and salad.

NUTRITION NOTES PER SERVING: calories 549 | protein 30.4 g | carbohydrate 11.8 g fat 42.7 g | saturated fat 20.85 g | fibre 1.4 g | added sugar none | salt 1.19 g

If you have time, allow the chicken to marinade in the korma sauce for up to 2 hours before cooking.

doodle spinach 'n'chicken noodle

This succulent and nutritious dish, with a hint of the Orient, cooks in a flash and tastes divine. If you've got greens instead of spinach, that'll do fine.

SERVES 2 | **PREPARATION: 10 MINS | COOKING TIME: 10 MINS**

175 g (6 oz) egg noodles
1 tablespoon sunflower oil
2 small boneless, skinless chicken breasts, thinly sliced diagonally
1 bunch salad onions, trimmed and halved widthways
1 garlic clove, sliced
100 g (4 oz) chestnut mushrooms, sliced
1½ teaspoons coarsely crushed black peppercorns
3 tablespoons oyster sauce
100 ml (3½ fl oz) chicken stock
100 g (4 oz) spinach leaves, cut into large strips (remove any tough stalks)
salt and pepper

Cook the noodles in boiling water for about 4 minutes, or according to the packet instructions. Drain well and keep warm.

Meanwhile, heat the sunflower oil in a frying pan then add the chicken slices, season and cook over a high heat for 3–4 minutes until browned and almost cooked through. Add the salad onions, garlic, mushrooms and crushed peppercorns to the pan and cook, stirring, for 2 minutes.

Add the oyster sauce and stock to the pan, stirring to heat through. Add the spinach leaves and cook for 1–2 minutes until just wilted. Stir and season with salt, then serve on a bed of noodles.

NUTRITION NOTES PER SERVING: calories 562 | protein 37 g | carbohydrate 70 g
fat 17 g | saturated fat 2 g | fibre 5 g | added sugar none | salt 3.81 g

ginger chicken with coconut rice

The delicious smells coming from the oven once this is on the go will drive your family's tastebuds wild.

SERVES 4 | **PREPARATION: 10 MINS | COOKING TIME: 25 MINS**

1 tablespoon vegetable oil
4 boneless chicken breasts, unskinned
2 tablespoons clear honey
1 tablespoon dark soy sauce
2 garlic cloves, crushed
2 cm (¾ in) piece root ginger, finely grated
grated rind and juice of 1 large orange
225 g (8 oz) button mushrooms, halved
2 bunches salad onions, trimmed and halved
50 g (2 oz) block creamed coconut, roughly chopped
200 g (7 oz) long-grain rice
1 bay leaf
orange wedges and bay leaves, to garnish

Pre-heat the oven to 190°C/375°F/gas 5.

Heat the oil in a frying pan and cook the chicken, skin-side down, for 2–3 minutes on each side until golden brown; transfer to an ovenproof dish. Mix together the honey, soy sauce, garlic, ginger and orange rind and juice, and pour over the chicken. Bake for 10 minutes, then add the mushrooms and salad onions, baste and bake for a further 10 minutes.

Meanwhile, make the coconut rice: bring 400 ml (14 fl oz) of water to the boil in a non-stick pan, add the creamed coconut and stir until it is dissolved; add the rice and bay leaf, cover and simmer for 12–15 minutes, stirring occasionally, until the rice is tender and the liquid absorbed. Serve with the chicken, garnished with orange wedges and bay leaves.

NUTRITION NOTES PER SERVING: calories 484 | protein 34 g | carbohydrate 56 g
fat 16 g | saturated fat 9 g | fibre 3 g | added sugar 8 g | salt 0.27 g

flash
chicken satay

I always serve chicken satay (the miniature variety) before we get down to the serious nosh, and the plate is empty in a flash. These scrummy skewers make a great main course and are delicious cooked over hot coals and served with a cold beer.

SERVES 2 | **PREPARATION: 15 MINS | COOKING TIME: 10 MINS**

200 g (7 oz) carton coconut cream
4 tablespoons crunchy
 peanut butter
1–2 teaspoons
 Worcestershire sauce
a few drops of Tabasco sauce
2 x 75 g (3 oz) boneless,
 skinless chicken breasts

1 lemon
1 carrot, cut into thin ribbons
1 mini cucumber,
 cut into thin ribbons
salt and pepper
25 g (1 oz) dry-roasted
 peanuts, roughly chopped, and
 2 warm naan breads, to serve

Pre-heat the oven to 200°C/400°F/gas 6. Pre-heat the grill to high.

Place the coconut cream and peanut butter in a bowl and beat together until well blended. Stir in the Worcestershire sauce and Tabasco. Sandwich the chicken breasts between plastic wrap then, using a rolling pin, bat them out as thinly as possible. Remove the plastic wrap and cut each breast in half lengthways.

Pour half the sauce into a shallow dish and add the chicken pieces, turning to coat them in the sauce. Thread on to skewers and cook under a hot grill for 4 minutes on each side until cooked through and well browned.

Gently heat the reserved satay sauce with a splash of water in a small pan. Place the naan in the oven to warm through.

Halve the lemon and squeeze the juice of one half into the warm satay sauce. Pile the carrot and cucumber ribbons on top of the warm naans and squeeze over the remaining lemon juice. Arrange the skewers on top and drizzle over the warm satay sauce.

NUTRITION NOTES PER SERVING: calories 1090 | protein 44.6 g | carbohydrate 80.4 g fat 66 g | saturated fat 33.79 g | fibre 5.7 g | added sugar 0.7 g | salt 2.15 g

chester's chicken chow mein

You can knock this up much quicker than the time it takes to get to the local take-away and back, and it tastes every bit as good. It's one of my dad's favourites, and he's always flabbergasted at how little time it takes – 'But you only just went to the kitchen!'

SERVES 2 **PREPARATION: 5 MINS | COOKING TIME: 10 MINS**

175 g (6 oz) egg noodles
1 tablespoon sunflower oil
1 onion, thinly sliced
2 garlic cloves, thinly sliced
1 cm (½ in) piece root ginger, finely chopped (optional)
100 g (4 oz) beansprouts
100 g (4 oz) mangetout, halved lengthways, or peas
175 g (6 oz) cooked chicken, shredded
1 tablespoon soy sauce
1 tablespoon sweet chilli sauce

Cook the noodles in a large pan of boiling, salted water, according to the packet instructions. Meanwhile, heat the oil in a wok or deep frying pan and stir-fry the onion over a high heat for 2–3 minutes until beginning to brown. Add the garlic, ginger (if using), beansprouts and mangetout or peas and stir-fry for 1 minute.

Drain the noodles well and add to the wok with the chicken and soy sauce and cook for 2 minutes until piping hot. Stir in the sweet chilli sauce and serve immediately.

NUTRITION NOTES PER SERVING: calories 616 | protein 41.2 g | carbohydrate 73.2 g
fat 19.6 g | saturated fat 2.9 g | fibre 5.5 g | added sugar none | salt 1.69 g

chiang mai thai mince

This puts a spicy spin on the traditional bolognese. For extra authenticity, serve with Thai fragrant rice.

SERVES 4 | **PREPARATION: 10 MINS | COOKING TIME: 15 MINS**

250 g (9 oz) long-grain or Thai fragrant rice
1 tablespoon vegetable oil
1 onion, halved and sliced
1 garlic clove, chopped
1 red pepper, cored, seeded and roughly chopped
450 g (1 lb) turkey or pork mince
½ teaspoon chilli powder
2 tablespoons dark soy sauce
175 ml (6 fl oz) chicken stock
2 teaspoons cornflour
a handful of fresh basil leaves
salt and pepper

Cook the rice in a pan of boiling water for about 15 minutes. Meanwhile, heat the oil in a pan and cook the onion for 3–4 minutes until golden. Stir in the garlic and pepper and cook for 4 minutes, then add the mince and chilli powder and cook for 2–3 minutes until well browned. Stir in the soy sauce and stock, bring to the boil and simmer for 5 minutes.

Blend the cornflour with 1 tablespoon of water until smooth, add to the pan and stir until slightly thickened; season with pepper and stir in the whole basil leaves. Drain the rice and spoon on to plates, top with the bolognese and serve.

NUTRITION NOTES PER SERVING: calories 413 | protein 30 g | carbohydrate 63 g fat 6 g | saturated fat 1 g | fibre 1 g | added sugar none | salt 0.33 g

For a richer taste, stir in 1 tablespoon of oyster sauce with the soy sauce and stock.

parma ham
turkey roulades

Turkey escalopes are delicious when wrapped in Parma ham – in fact, any cured ham will do, or you could even use thinly sliced smoked bacon.

SERVES 4   **PREPARATION: 10 MINS | COOKING TIME 10 MINS**

4 x 150 g (5 oz) turkey escalopes
2 garlic cloves, finely chopped
grated rind and juice of 1 lemon
2 tablespoons chopped fresh basil or chives
4 slices Parma ham
2 tablespoons olive oil
salt and pepper
mixed salad and freshly cooked pasta or crusty Italian bread, to serve

Halve each turkey escalope horizontally and open out. Season the flesh well and sprinkle over the garlic, lemon rind and chopped herbs, then sandwich the pieces back together again. Wrap each escalope in a slice of Parma ham and pin in place with cocktail sticks.

Heat the olive oil in a frying pan and cook the turkey for 4–5 minutes until golden brown. Turn over, drizzle with the lemon juice and cook for a further 3–4 minutes until cooked through. Serve with salad and pasta or warm, crusty, sun-dried tomato bread.

NUTRITION NOTES PER SERVING: calories 261 | protein 42.8 g | carbohydrate 0.7 g fat 9.6 g | saturated fat 2.22 g | fibre 0.1 g | added sugar none | salt 1.62 g

peking duck

When I go to a Chinese restaurant I particularly enjoy the sociability involved in eating Peking duck. It was a real challenge coming up with a quick version, as it normally takes hours to prepare.

SERVES 2 | **PREPARATION: 10 MINS | COOKING TIME 10 MINS**

2 x 175 g (6 oz) duck breasts
1 tablespoon dark soy sauce
2 tablespoons clear honey
1 teaspoon Chinese five-
  spice powder
¼ teaspoon coarse black pepper
1 tablespoon sunflower oil

FOR THE PLUM SAUCE
1 teaspoon sesame oil
1 garlic clove, crushed
1 tablespoon white wine vinegar

1 tablespoon soy sauce
3 tablespoons plum jam
1 pinch dried chilli flakes

TO SERVE
10 Chinese-style
  pancakes, warmed
4 salad onions, shredded
10 cm (4 in) piece cucumber,
  cut into matchsticks
2 tablespoons fresh coriander
  leaves, plus sprigs, to serve

Halve the duck breasts horizontally, then cut each piece lengthways into very thin strips. Stir together the soy sauce, honey, five-spice powder and pepper; pour over the duck and set aside to marinate for a few minutes. Meanwhile, heat the sesame oil in a small pan and gently cook the garlic for 1 minute without colouring, then stir in the vinegar, soy sauce, jam and chilli flakes. Cook for 2 minutes, stirring until well blended and warmed through. Pass the sauce through a fine sieve into a small serving dish. Drain the duck strips. Heat the sunflower oil in a wok or deep frying pan and stir fry the duck over a high heat for 2–3 minutes until well browned. To serve, spread the warm pancakes with a little of the plum sauce and top with a few strips of duck, salad onion and cucumber. Sprinkle over some coriander leaves and roll up. Garnish with coriander sprigs and serve.

NUTRITION NOTES PER SERVING: calories 1139 | protein 26.3 g | carbohydrate 52.9 g fat 92.8 g | saturated fat 26.4 g | fibre 1.2 g | added sugar 34.7 g | salt 2.83 g

To warm the pancakes through, place them on a heatproof plate, cover with foil and sit over a pan of gently simmering water for 4–5 minutes.

POULTRY

succulent spiced duckling

This is a very stylish meal, perfect for special occasions – it looks impressive but is really simple to make. It goes down beautifully with a nice spicy red wine.

SERVES 2 | **PREPARATION: 15 MINS | COOKING TIME: 25 MINS**

2 x 100 g (4 oz) duckling breasts
1 teaspoon mixed spice
½ teaspoon cayenne pepper
½ teaspoon salt

FOR THE CABBAGE
a knob of butter
225 g (8 oz) red cabbage, shredded
1 small red onion, thinly sliced
1 tart apple, peeled and diced

2 tablespoons light
   muscovado sugar
¼ teaspoon ground cinnamon
120 ml (4 fl oz) red wine
juice of 1 orange
4 tablespoons soured cream
handful chopped fresh herbs, such
   as basil, parsley, coriander, chives
salt and pepper

Score the duck skin in a lattice pattern. Mix the spices and salt in a shallow bowl and add the duck; using your fingertips, rub in the spices.

Cook the duck skin-side down in a hot griddle pan or frying pan for 7 minutes on each side until browned and cooked through but still a little pink in the centre. Remove from the pan and place on a warm plate to rest for 5 minutes.

Meanwhile, melt the butter in a wok or deep frying pan and stir-fry the cabbage over a high heat for 1–2 minutes. Add the red onion and apple and cook for a further 1–2 minutes. Stir in the sugar and cinnamon and cook, stirring, until the sugar dissolves. Add the wine and orange juice and simmer gently for 10 minutes until tender.

Meanwhile, stir together the soured cream and fresh herbs and season to taste. Spoon the cabbage onto serving plates. Slice the duck breasts and fan out on top of the cabbage, top with a spoonful of herby cream and serve immediately.

NUTRITION NOTES PER SERVING: calories 674 | protein 14.7 g | carbohydrate 25 g fat 53.5 g | saturated fat 18.03 g | fibre 4.7 g | added sugar 5.2 | salt 1.85 g

spiced shish skewers

I bet you can't say that after a few glasses of wine! As for the dip, it's simply a combination of cucumber and tomato, but that doesn't sound half as exciting or sexy as it tastes. This dish is also super served cold.

SERVES 4 | **PREPARATION: 15 MINS | COOKING TIME: 15 MINS**

450 g (1 lb) minced lamb
1 small onion, finely chopped
3 tablespoons chopped fresh mint
1 tablespoon each chopped fresh oregano and parsley
½ teaspoon each mixed spice, ground coriander and ground cumin
450 g (1 lb) small new potatoes
½ small cucumber
150 g (5 oz) carton natural yogurt
1 tomato, seeded and diced
¼ teaspoon garlic powder or 1 garlic clove, crushed
salt and pepper
4 pitta breads, plus wedges of cucumber, tomato and lemon, to serve

Pre-heat the grill to high. Mix together the lamb, onion, 1 tablespoon of mint, the oregano, parsley, mixed spice, coriander and cumin and season with salt and pepper. Divide the mixture into 12 and squeeze around 12 skewers.

Cook the potatoes in boiling, salted water for 10–15 minutes or until tender.

Grill the lamb kebabs for 8–10 minutes, turning occasionally until well browned. Meanwhile, grate the cucumber, squeeze out the excess liquid with your hands and mix with the yogurt, tomato, 1 tablespoon of mint, the garlic and the salt and pepper.

Drain the potatoes and toss with the remaining mint. Serve the lamb with potatoes, pitta bread, a dollop of the yogurt and wedges of fresh cucumber and tomato. Oh – and a wedge of lemon, too!

NUTRITION NOTES PER SERVING: calories 393 | protein 25 g | carbohydrate 25 g fat 22 g | saturated fat 11 g | fibre 2 g | added sugar none | salt 0.52 g

MEAT

lazy luscious lamb biryani

The classic biryani is a festive casserole of rice and meat. Traditionally, the grains of rice are yellow and white, the yellow provided by saffron mixed with milk then drizzled over the top of the rice before cooking. If you're feeling posh, why not replace the turmeric with a few strands of saffron – the cooking aroma and taste are exceptional.

SERVES 4   **PREPARATION: 10 MINS | COOKING TIME: 20 MINS**

1 teaspoon each ground
   turmeric and cumin
½ teaspoon each ground
   coriander and chilli powder
2 tablespoons vegetable oil
250 g (9 oz) lean, boneless
   lamb, cubed
15 g (½ oz) butter
1 onion, sliced
2 garlic cloves, chopped

1 cinnamon stick, halved
225 g (8 oz) basmati rice
600 ml (1 pint) hot chicken
   or vegetable stock
350 g (12 oz) small
   cauliflower florets
100 g (4 oz) peas
salt and pepper
toasted flaked almonds, to garnish

Mix together the turmeric, cumin, coriander, chilli and 1 tablespoon of the oil. Toss the lamb in the mixture to coat.

Heat the butter and remaining oil in a pan and cook the onion and garlic for 4–5 minutes until softened. Add the cinnamon and lamb and cook over a high heat for 3 minutes.

Stir in the rice and stock and bring to the boil. Add the cauliflower, cover and simmer gently for 8–10 minutes until the rice is almost tender. Stir in the peas and cook for a further 2–3 minutes until the stock has been absorbed. Remove the cinnamon stick, season to taste and serve garnished with the toasted flaked almonds.

NUTRITION NOTES PER SERVING: calories 459 | protein 23.7 g | carbohydrate 55 g fat 17.5 g | saturated fat 5.41 g | fibre 3.5 g | added sugar none | salt 0.99 g

snappy lamb hot pot

In northern England the hot pot was a tall, earthenware pot. Mutton chops were stacked round the sides, the veggies in the middle, and a dozen oysters were slipped in on special occasions before it was finished off with a layer of sliced potatoes and baked for two to three hours. But with my version you really can cook a delicious, classic hot pot in less than half an hour.

SERVES 4 | **PREPARATION: 15 MINS | COOKING TIME 25 MINS**

4 x 100 g (4 oz) trimmed
   lean lamb steaks
2 tablespoons olive oil
1 onion, sliced
1 garlic clove, sliced
400 g (14 oz) can
   chopped tomatoes
120 ml (4 fl oz) hot chicken or
   vegetable stock

100 g (4 oz) green beans, halved
½ teaspoon mixed dried herbs
few drops Tabasco or chilli sauce
500 g (1 lb 2 oz) par-boiled
   potatoes, very thinly sliced
a knob of butter
salt and pepper

Cut each piece of lamb lengthways into two or three strips. Heat the oil in a large sauté pan or a frying pan with a lid and cook the onion, garlic and lamb for 3–4 minutes until well browned.

Stir in the tomatoes, stock, beans and herbs and bring to the boil; add Tabasco, salt and pepper to taste.

Arrange the potatoes in overlapping layers on top of the meat. Season, cover and simmer for 15 minutes until the potato is tender.

Pre-heat the grill to high. Dot the potatoes with butter and place under the grill for 2–3 minutes until nicely browned.

NUTRITION NOTES PER SERVING: calories 355 | protein 25.2 g | carbohydrate 27.7 g
fat 16.8 g | saturated fat 6.29 g | fibre 3.3 g | added sugar none | salt 0.93 g

To par-boil potatoes, cook them whole, or halved if they are large, in a pan of boiling water for 10 minutes, or until they are almost tender. Drain and cool before continuing with the recipe.

MEAT

joy soy lamb and ginger rice

I'm particularly fond of lamb. Perhaps it's something to do with its subtle sweetness. This dish is full of Oriental flavours and style.

| SERVES 4 | PREPARATION: 10 MINS \| COOKING TIME: 30 MINS |

1 teaspoon ground fennel or cumin

1 garlic clove, crushed

1 tablespoon chopped fresh
  rosemary, or 1 teaspoon
  dried rosemary

1 teaspoon each grated lemon
  rind and juice

3 tablespoons olive oil

1 tablespoon soy sauce

1 onion, sliced

2 garlic cloves, finely chopped

2 cm (¾ in) piece root ginger,
  finely chopped

200 g (7 oz) long-grain rice

100 g (4 oz) button
  mushrooms, sliced

450 ml (15 fl oz) hot
  vegetable stock

½ teaspoon ground turmeric

4 x 100 g (4 oz) boneless chump,
  leg or shoulder lamb steaks

2 tablespoons chopped
  fresh coriander or parsley

salt and pepper

½ cucumber, seeded and cut
  into strips, to garnish

Stir together the fennel or cumin, garlic, rosemary, lemon rind and juice, 2 tablespoons of the oil and the soy sauce; set aside.

Heat the remaining oil in a pan and cook the onion, garlic and ginger for 4–5 minutes until softened and golden. Stir in the rice and cook, stirring, for 1 minute. Add the mushrooms, stock and turmeric and bring to the boil. Cover and simmer gently for 15 minutes until the liquid is absorbed and the rice is tender.

Pre-heat the grill to high. Brush the lamb with the soy sauce mix, then grill for 4 minutes; turn, brush with more soy sauce mixture and cook for 3–4 minutes longer until crispy and tender. Stir the coriander or parsley into the rice and season. Spoon the rice onto serving plates, slice the lamb into strips and arrange on top of the rice. Garnish with fine strips of cucumber.

NUTRITION NOTES PER SERVING: calories 527 | protein 23.1 g | carbohydrate 48.5 g fat 28.1 g | saturated fat 10.67 g | fibre 0.9 g | added sugar none | salt 1.31 g

MEAT

jazz and spice shepherd's pie

Shepherd's pie is such a lovely old-fashioned dish – here I've jazzed it up to great effect with a touch of spicy curry paste.

SERVES 2-3 | **PREPARATION: 10 MINS | COOKING TIME: 20 MINS**

450 g (1 lb) floury potatoes, diced
2 tablespoons sunflower oil
1 small onion, finely chopped
1 garlic clove, finely chopped
1 large carrot, diced
300 g (10 oz) minced lamb
2 tablespoons mild curry paste
250 ml (8 fl oz) hot lamb stock
1 tablespoon tomato ketchup

2 teaspoons dark soy sauce
1 teaspoon cornflour
50 g (2 oz) frozen peas, thawed
2 tomatoes, roughly chopped
2 tablespoons milk
a knob of butter
25 g (1 oz) mature Cheddar, grated
salt and pepper

Cook the potatoes in a large pan of boiling, salted water for 8–10 minutes until tender.

Heat 1 tablespoon of sunflower oil in a large frying pan and cook the onion, garlic, carrot and mince for 3–4 minutes until well browned. Stir in the curry paste, stock, tomato ketchup and soy sauce. Bring to the boil and simmer rapidly for 3–4 minutes. Mix the cornflour to a paste with a little water and stir into the pan with the peas and chopped tomatoes and bring back to the boil, stirring, until slightly thickened. Season with salt and pepper to taste.

Drain the potatoes well and return to the pan. Mash well, then beat in the milk and butter until smooth and creamy; season to taste.

Pre-heat the grill to medium. Spoon the mince mixture into a heatproof pie dish and spoon over the mashed potato. Using a fork, mark a criss-cross pattern on the top.

Sprinkle over the Cheddar and place under a medium grill for 3 minutes until the cheese melts and the pie is speckled with brown. Spoon onto plates and serve.

NUTRITION NOTES PER SERVING: calories 864 | protein 40.6 g | carbohydrate 60.4 g fat 52.6 g | saturated fat 21.87 g | fibre 10.6 g | added sugar 1 g | salt 2.08 g

grilled peppery pork and apple

Perk up your pork with my peppery coating.

SERVES 4	PREPARATION: 10 MINS	COOKING TIME: 10 MINS

400 g (14 oz) pork fillet, cut into 12 x 2 cm (¾ in) thick slices
1½ teaspoons freshly ground black pepper
½ teaspoon paprika
grated rind of 1 lemon
1 teaspoon fresh lemon juice
4 tablespoons olive oil
2 apples, unpeeled
300 g (10 oz) Savoy cabbage, finely shredded
1 garlic clove, finely chopped
150 ml (5 fl oz) vegetable stock
200 ml carton crème fraîche
salt and pepper

Pre-heat the grill to high. Place the pork slices between two layers of plastic wrap, then press down with the palm of your hand to flatten the meat out to a thickness of about 6 mm (¼ in). Remove the plastic wrap.

In a bowl, mix together the pepper, paprika, lemon rind and juice and 3 tablespoons of the oil. Slice each apple widthways into four slices. Drizzle the oil mixture over one side of the pork and apple slices. Grill the pork slices for 4–5 minutes on each side, turning once. Grill the apple slices, on the oiled side only, for about 5 minutes until cooked. Keep the pork and apple slices warm.

Meanwhile, heat the remaining oil in a large frying pan. Add the cabbage and garlic and cook, covered, for 4–5 minutes until just tender. Stir in the stock and the crème fraîche, warm through briefly, season to taste, then spoon onto warmed serving plates. Top with the pork slices and serve the apple slices on the side or on top.

NUTRITION NOTES PER SERVING: calories 454 | protein 23 g | carbohydrate 14 g
fat 34 g | saturated fat 14 g | fibre 3 g | added sugar none | salt 1.08 g

canton stir-fried beef with noodles

What came first – Chinese noodles or Italian spaghetti? The argument will go on for another 100 years. This Cantonese dish is one of the quickest and tastiest around – guaranteed to have you wok-ing. Yes, owright Ainsley . . .

SERVES 2　　PREPARATION: 10 MINS | COOKING TIME: 5 MINS

250 g (9 oz) tender beef steak cut
　into 1 cm (½ in) wide strips
1 tablespoon soy sauce
1 tablespoon dry sherry
1 tablespoon hoisin sauce
2 tablespoons cornflour
2 tablespoons sunflower oil, plus
　extra for deep frying
25 g (1 oz) cellophane (sometimes
　labelled 'stir-fry' noodles)
　or rice noodles
100g/4 oz pak choi leaves or
　broccoli florets

1 red pepper, seeded and sliced
handful fresh basil leaves,
　roughly torn
salt and pepper

FOR THE SAUCE
4 tablespoons dry sherry
2 tablespoons light soy sauce
1 teaspoon sesame oil
1 tablespoon clear honey
1 teaspoon hot chilli sauce
cooked Thai-style fragrant rice,
　to serve

Place the beef strips in a bowl with the soy sauce, sherry, hoisin sauce and cornflour; mix well and set aside. Deep fry the noodles in hot oil for 30 seconds until puffed and white. Remove with a slotted spoon and drain on kitchen paper.

To make the sauce stir together the sherry, soy sauce, sesame oil, honey and hot chilli sauce. Heat a little oil in a wok and stir-fry the beef, making sure you add the juices from the marinade, too, for 1 minute. Add the pak choi and pepper and cook for 2 minutes. Add the sauce and cook for a further 2 minutes until the meat is tender; stir in the basil and check the seasoning.

Divide the rice between two serving plates and spoon over the spicy beef mixture. Top with the crispy noodles and serve immediately.

NUTRITION NOTES PER SERVING: calories 698 | protein 29.3 g | carbohydrate 58.1 g fat 35.6 g | saturated fat 5.97 g | fibre 1.9 g | added sugar 12.3 g | salt 1.86 g

joe's bake and glaze sticky ribs

A good, quick recipe for spare ribs that my nephew Joe always insists on when he comes to supper. He loves the sucking, licking and picking of these sticky ribs. Time to get glazing! PS Serve with plenty of paper napkins.

SERVES 4   PREPARATION: 10 MINS | COOKING TIME 40 MINS

1 kg (2 lb 4 oz) pork spare ribs
1 onion, sliced
1 teaspoon dried mixed herbs
5 tablespoons tomato ketchup
3 tablespoons apple or orange juice
75g (3 oz) dark muscovado sugar
1 tablespoon English mustard
3 tablespoons Worcestershire sauce
½–1 teaspoon Tabasco sauce
550g (1 lb 4 oz) potatoes, cut into wedges
1 tablespoon olive oil
salt and pepper
mixed salad leaves and cherry tomato halves, to serve

Preheat the oven to 200°C/400°F/gas 6. Place the ribs, onion and herbs in a large pan and cover with water. Bring to the boil, then lower the heat and simmer for 20 minutes.

Meanwhile, in a bowl, mix the tomato ketchup, fruit juice, sugar, mustard, Worcestershire and Tabasco sauces, and salt and pepper. Steam the potatoes for 10 minutes.

Using a slotted spoon, place the spare ribs in a single layer in a shallow ovenproof dish and spoon over the glaze. Place the potatoes on a baking sheet, brush with olive oil and season. Bake the meat and potatoes for 20 minutes until the meat is tender and the potatoes crisp. Serve with salad leaves and cherry tomatoes.

NUTRITION NOTES PER SERVING: calories 849 | protein 30 g | carbohydrate 53 g fat 59 g | saturated fat 23 g | fibre 2 g | added sugar 22 g | salt 1.11 g

spice brit's pork chop chow

Succulent pork with fresh beetroot chutney and creamy garlic potatoes. This combination works so well that you'll be getting requests for a repeat performance.

SERVES 4 | **PREPARATION: 10 MINS | COOKING TIME: 20 MINS**

450g (1 lb) small new potatoes
25 g (1 oz) butter
1 onion, chopped
250 g (9 oz) cooked
  beetroot, coarsely grated
2 tablespoons cider vinegar
½ teaspoon ground ginger
grated rind and juice of 1 orange
25 g (1 oz) raisins

2 teaspoons light
  muscovado sugar
4 x 150 g (5 oz) pork
  loin chops with bone
1 teaspoon English mustard
6 tablespoons double cream
1 garlic clove, crushed
1 tablespoon snipped fresh chives
salt and pepper

Cook the potatoes in lightly salted boiling water for 15 minutes or until tender. Meanwhile, melt the butter in a pan, add the onion and cook for 3–4 minutes until golden. Stir in the beetroot, vinegar, ginger, the orange rind and juice, raisins and sugar. Cover and simmer for 5 minutes or until softened.

Pre-heat the grill to high. Season the chops and brush with a little mustard. Grill for about 4–5 minutes on each side until cooked through but still moist and juicy.

Drain the potatoes. Gently heat the cream and garlic in a frying pan, then stir in the potatoes and chives; season to taste. Spoon onto serving plates and top with grilled pork chops; serve with the beetroot chutney.

NUTRITION NOTES PER SERVING: calories 679 | protein 27.9 g | carbohydrate 36.2 g fat 47.9 g | saturated fat 24.27 g | fibre 3 g | added sugar 2.6 g | salt 0.84 g

MEAT

144

chilli-jam gammon

You can't beat the taste of a juicy gammon steak, and it's especially delicious with my sweet chilli-jam sauce and crispy corn fritters. You can use a tin of creamed sweetcorn instead, but add one less egg and no milk.

SERVES 2   **PREPARATION: 10 MINS | COOKING TIME: 20 MINS**

2 x 175 g (6 oz) smoked
  gammon steaks
1–2 tablespoons sunflower oil
1 onion, finely chopped
2 garlic cloves, finely chopped
2 red chillies, seeded and
  finely chopped
juice of 1 orange
1 tablespoon clear honey
1 tablespoon malt vinegar
2 tablespoons tomato ketchup

FOR THE FRITTERS
2 eggs
4 tablespoons milk
50 g (2 oz) self-raising flour
25 g (1 oz) cornflour
275 g (10 oz) can
  sweetcorn, drained
vegetable oil for frying
salt and pepper

Brush the gammon steaks with a little oil and cook under a hot grill or in a frying pan for 3–4 minutes on each side until cooked through.

Meanwhile, make the jam: heat the remaining oil in a small pan, add the onion and cook for 2–3 minutes. Add the garlic and chillies and cook for a further 2 minutes until softened. Stir in the orange juice, honey, vinegar and tomato ketchup and simmer gently for 5 minutes.

To make the corn fritters crack the eggs into a large bowl and whisk in the milk and both flours to make a smooth batter. Stir in the sweetcorn and plenty of seasoning. Cook large spoonfuls of the sweetcorn mixture in a hot, oiled frying pan for 3–4 minutes on each side until crisp and golden; repeat to make six pancakes.

Place the gammon and sweetcorn fritters on a plate, spoon over a little dollop of the chilli jam and serve.

NUTRITION NOTES PER SERVING: calories 963 | protein 66.6 g | carbohydrate 75.1 g fat 46.1 g | saturated fat 12.59 g | fibre 3.6 g | added sugar 18.3 g | salt 12.37 g

french-style pork with root purée

Ooh la-la! This *chic* supper has plenty of French flair and presents beautifully. Unlike any other recipe in this book, however, this dish does need a little forward planning, as the prunes need soaking in advance to suck up the wine for plumpness and flavour.

SERVES 2 | **PREPARATION: 10 MINS | COOKING TIME: 15 MINS**

FOR THE MASH
225 g (8 oz) parsnips, cubed
225 g (8 oz) floury potatoes, cubed
3–4 tablespoons milk
40 g (1½ oz) butter
salt and freshly ground pepper

FOR THE PORK
225 g (8 oz) tenderloin pork fillet,
    cut into 1 cm (½ in) slices

1 tablespoon flour, seasoned with
    salt and pepper
50 g (2 oz) butter
8 ready-to-eat prunes soaked for at
    least 30 mins in 150 ml (5 fl oz)
    dry white wine
1 tablespoon redcurrant or
    cranberry jelly
150 ml (5 fl oz) double cream
juice of ½ lemon
salt and pepper

Cook the parsnips and potatoes in a large pan of boiling, salted water for 10–12 minutes until tender. Dust the pork with the seasoned flour, shaking off any excess. Heat half the butter in a large frying pan and, when foaming, cook the pork for 1–2 minutes on each side. Remove and set aside.

Strain the wine into the hot pan and bring to the boil. Stir in the redcurrant jelly and cook for a further 2 minutes, stirring until melted. Add the cream, prunes and pork, season to taste and simmer gently for 2–3 minutes until the pork is cooked through.

Drain the root vegetables and mash well. Add the milk and remaining butter and whizz with an electric hand whisk until smooth and puréed; season to taste.

Squeeze a little lemon juice into the pork pan and check the seasoning. Pile the mash onto serving plates and spoon over the pork mixture.

NUTRITION NOTES PER SERVING: calories 1149 | protein 32 g | carbohydrate 63.5 g fat 83.4 g | saturated fat 49.47 g | fibre 9.2 g | added sugar 5.2 g | salt 1.89 g

The prunes can be soaked for up to 8 hours, so pop them into the wine before you go to work, and they'll be ready when you get home.

MEAT

pasta cream
bean dream

A rhyming seasonal spaghetti dish that is poetry on the plate.

| SERVES 4 | PREPARATION: 5 MINS | COOKING TIME: 15 MINS |

300 g (11 oz) spaghetti
300 g (11 oz) runner beans, sliced on the diagonal
1 tablespoon olive oil
1 onion, sliced
6 rashers streaky bacon, cut into strips
200 g (7 oz) half-fat crème fraîche
3 tablespoons vegetable stock
1 Little Gem lettuce, finely shredded
salt and pepper
freshly grated Parmesan, to serve

Cook the spaghetti in a large pan of boiling, salted water, according to the packet instructions, adding the runner beans for the last 4 minutes of cooking time.

Meanwhile, heat the oil in a frying pan and cook the onion and bacon for 5 minutes until nicely browned. Stir in the crème fraîche and stock and simmer gently for 1 minute, without boiling.

Drain the spaghetti and beans and return to the pan. Stir in the crème fraîche sauce and shredded lettuce and season to taste. Transfer to serving plates and sprinkle with Parmesan and plenty of freshly ground black pepper.

NUTRITION NOTES PER SERVING: calories 496 | protein 20 g | carbohydrate 64 g
fat 20 g | saturated fat 7 g | fibre 4 g | added sugar none | salt 1.77 g

You can use another type of pasta, such as tagliatelle or linguine, instead of spaghetti.

marvellous chilli-cheese meatballs

My meatballs are marvellous! Well, so the wife keeps telling me. What do you think? I've made them with pork, but any lean mince will do just as well. You could also serve the meatballs with other types of pasta, like linguine, spaghettini, tagliatelle, taglioni or fettucine, to name but a few.

SERVES 2 | **PREPARATION: 10 MINS | COOKING TIME: 20 MINS**

225 g (8 oz) lean minced pork
4 salad onions, finely chopped
2 garlic cloves, finely chopped
1 red chilli, seeded and
  finely chopped
2 tablespoons freshly grated
  Parmesan, plus extra to serve
2 teaspoons fresh thyme leaves

1 tablespoon olive oil
100 ml (3½ fl oz) red wine
150 g (5 oz) spaghetti or tagliatelle
400 g (14 oz) can chopped tomatoes
1 dried bay leaf
pinch of sugar
salt and pepper

Mix together the mince, salad onions, garlic, chilli, Parmesan, thyme and plenty of salt and pepper. Shape into 12 small, firm balls. Heat the oil in a large pan and cook the meatballs for 3–4 minutes, shaking the pan frequently, until well browned. Pour in the red wine and bubble vigorously for 1–2 minutes.

Cook the pasta in a large pan of boiling, salted water according to packet instructions. Stir the chopped tomatoes, bay leaf, sugar and salt and pepper into the meatballs; bring to the boil and simmer for 8–10 minutes until the meatballs are cooked through.

Drain the pasta and return to the pan; spoon in some of the tomato sauce and toss well together. Transfer to large serving bowls and spoon over the chilli-cheese meatballs with the sauce; sprinkle liberally with Parmesan and serve.

NUTRITION NOTES PER SERVING: calories 587 | protein 38.3 g | carbohydrate 64.4 g
fat 17.7 g | saturated fat 5.42 g | fibre 4 g | added sugar 0.5 g | salt 0.89

pavarotti pasta

I'm sure you've heard of the three tenors; well, this is the three cheeses – and when you taste this dish, you'll be singing their praises. 'Nice aroma, nice aroma.' Well, what can you find that rhymes with *'Nessun dorma'*?

SERVES 4 | **PREPARATION: 5 MINS | COOKING TIME: 15 MINS**

350 g (12 oz) pasta shapes, such as penne or fusilli
6 rashers rindless streaky bacon, chopped
100 g (4 oz) Mozzarella, finely chopped
75 g (3 oz) Cheddar, grated
50 g (2 oz) Parmesan, grated
150 ml (5 fl oz) single cream
2–3 tablespoons milk (optional)
salt and pepper
green salad leaves, to serve

Cook the pasta in a pan of boiling salted water for about 12 minutes, according to the packet instructions.

Meanwhile, heat a small frying pan, then cook the bacon until crispy. Drain on kitchen paper.

Drain the pasta and return it to the pan. Stir in the Mozzarella, Cheddar, Parmesan and cream and cook over a low heat, stirring, for 1–2 minutes, until the sauce is just warmed through. If the sauce is too thick, thin it by adding a little milk. Season with salt and pepper to taste.

Arrange the salad leaves on four serving plates. Spoon the pasta in creamy sauce on top, and serve sprinkled with the crispy bacon bits. Wash down with a bottle of Cava.

NUTRITION NOTES PER SERVING: calories 772 | protein 34 g | carbohydrate 68 g
fat 42 g | saturated fat 22 g | fibre 3 g | added sugar none | salt 3.09 g

my maddie's spicy sausages

My kids and I love to shape up these sausage treats and like to eat them USA style with spicy potato wedges and a tasty smoky sauce.

SERVES 4   PREPARATION: 15 MINS | COOKING TIME: 15 MINS

FOR THE PATTIES
450 g (1 lb) herby sausages
4 salad onions, finely chopped
1 tablespoon cranberry sauce
2 tablespoons flour, seasoned with
  salt and pepper
1 tablespoon sunflower oil

FOR THE POTATO WEDGES
4 x 200 g (7 oz) baking potatoes,
  cooked and cooled
1-2 tablespoons olive oil

¼ teaspoon salt
¼ teaspoon ground cumin
a pinch of cayenne

SMOKY SAUCE
juice of 1 orange
1 tablespoon clear honey
1 tablespoon malt vinegar
2 tablespoons tomato ketchup
1 tablespoon dark soy sauce
1 teaspoon English mustard

To make the patties, skin the sausages and mix with the salad onions, cranberry sauce and plenty of seasoning. Shape the mixture into eight sausage shapes then dust with the seasoned flour. Heat the sunflower oil in a large frying pan and cook the patties for 5–6 minutes on each side until well browned and cooked through.

Make the potato wedges: cut each potato into eight wedges and brush with the olive oil. Stir together the salt, cumin and cayenne and sprinkle over the wedges. Brush a griddle pan or large frying pan with a little more oil and cook the wedges for 3–4 minutes on each side until crisp and golden.

Meanwhile, make the smoky sauce: in a small pan heat together the orange juice, honey, vinegar, ketchup, soy sauce and mustard; bring to the boil and simmer rapidly for 2–3 minutes until slightly thickened. Arrange the patties and potato wedges on serving plates and spoon over a dollop of the smoky sauce. Great with some nice fresh lemonade. Yes please Dad!

NUTRITION NOTES PER SERVING: calories 689 | protein 17.3 g | carbohydrate 63.8 g fat 42.2 g | saturated fat 14.65 g | fibre 3.5 g | added sugar 8.4 g | salt 3.36 g

This dish is great served with crispy onion rings. Simply slice a large onion into rings and soak in a little milk for 10–15 minutes. Drain well, dust with seasoned flour and deep fry until crisp and golden – delicious!

MEAT

double-quick caroline's cassoulet

Cassoulet, like paella, can be made in many different styles. Goose or duck confits and sausages with bacon or salt pork or lamb are all delicious. It can take up to three days to prepare, but here is my own double-quick version. It's my producer, Caroline's, favourite nibble.

SERVES 4   PREPARATION: 10 MINS | COOKING TIME: 40 MINS

1 tablespoon olive oil
1 onion, chopped
2 garlic cloves, finely chopped
250 g (9 oz) each cubed lamb or pork
6 rashers smoked streaky bacon, roughly chopped
400 g (14 oz) can tomatoes
2 carrots, diced
150 ml (5 fl oz) red wine
150 ml (5 fl oz) pint lamb stock
1 teaspoon each fresh, or ¼ teaspoon each dried, rosemary, thyme and parsley
400 g (14 oz) can haricot beans, drained
2 tablespoons fresh white breadcrumbs
salt and pepper
chopped fresh parsley, to garnish

Heat the oil in a large pan and cook the onion and garlic for 3–4 minutes until softened. Add the lamb or pork and bacon and stir-fry for 5 minutes.

Stir in the tomatoes, carrots, wine, stock and herbs, then cover and cook over a medium heat for 20–25 minutes until the meat is tender.

Pre-heat the grill to high. Stir the beans into the pan, season with salt and pepper and transfer to a heatproof serving dish. Sprinkle over the breadcrumbs, then grill for a few minutes until the topping is golden. Sprinkle with the chopped parsley and serve with a nice fresh red wine.

NUTRITION NOTES PER SERVING: calories 520 | protein 38 g | carbohydrate 23 g
fat 28 g | saturated fat 11 g | fibre 6 g | added sugar none | salt 2.3 g

MEAT

156

mustard basil beef rolls

Beef and mustard is a fantastic combination; this dish also tastes great using that other classic accompaniment, creamed horseradish, in place of the mustard.

SERVES 2 **PREPARATION: 10 MINS | COOKING TIME: 15 MINS**

2 x 175 g (6 oz) sirloin steaks, trimmed
1 tablespoon English mustard
2 garlic cloves, crushed
4 tablespoons chopped fresh basil or parsley
1 teaspoon cracked black peppercorns
25 g (1 oz) butter, at room temperature
1 tablespoon olive oil
1 small onion, finely chopped
2 tablespoons brandy
150 ml (5 fl oz) double cream
pinch of caster sugar
salt and pepper
steamed new potatoes or mash and steamed, buttered cabbage, to serve

Place the steaks on a sheet of plastic wrap and cover with another sheet. Bat out with a rolling pin until 6 mm (¼ in) thick. Remove the plastic wrap. Mix together the mustard, garlic, half the basil or parsley, pepper and butter until well blended. Spread the mixture onto the steaks, roll up tightly and secure with string or cocktail sticks.

Heat the oil in a frying pan and cook the steaks for 6–8 minutes, turning frequently until well browned. Remove the steaks from the pan, cover and rest for 3–4 minutes. Add the onion to the steak pan and cook for 2 minutes until beginning to soften. Stir in the brandy and bubble vigorously for 1 minute. Stir in the cream and heat through for 1–2 minutes. Season with salt, pepper and caster sugar to taste, and stir in the remaining basil or parsley.

Remove the string or cocktail sticks and serve the beef roulades with your choice of potatoes, buttered cabbage and creamy basil sauce.

NUTRITION NOTES PER SERVING: calories 877 | protein 33.3 g | carbohydrate 9.9 g fat 74.7 g | saturated fat 39.65 g | fibre 0.7 g | added sugar 0.5 g | salt 1.35 g

MEAT

158

beefburgers with blue cheese sauce

I always find a tasty beefburger a hard thing to turn down. And these are really easy to make and have a lovely, juicy texture . . . yum!

SERVES 2 | **PREPARATION: 10 MINS | COOKING TIME: 10 MINS**

250 g (9 oz) lean beef mince
4 small gherkins, finely chopped
3 tablespoons chopped fresh parsley
1 egg yolk
1 tablespoon sunflower oil
1 tablespoon Dijon mustard
2 tablespoons mayonnaise
50 g (2 oz) blue cheese such as Stilton or Gorgonzola, crumbled
salt and pepper
seeded burger buns, shredded lettuce and sliced tomato, to serve

Mix together the mince, gherkins, parsley, egg yolk and plenty of salt and pepper. Shape the mixture into even-sized burgers.

Brush the burgers with a little oil and cook in a hot frying pan for 3–4 minutes on each side until well browned but still a little pink in the centre.

Meanwhile, stir together the mustard and mayonnaise then gently fold in the blue cheese.

Serve the burgers in seeded buns with plenty of salad and a good dollop of the blue cheese dressing.

NUTRITION NOTES PER SERVING: calories 516 | protein 34 g | carbohydrate 1.6 g
fat 41.6 g | saturated fat 11.83 g | fibre 0.9 g | added sugar none | salt 1.74 g

MEAT

peppered nugget steak

I cook this dish time and again when I'm entertaining – it makes a lovely dinner-party main course.

SERVES 2 | **PREPARATION: 15 MINS | COOKING TIME: 15 MINS**

2 x 150 g (5 oz) beef medallions
2 tablespoons cracked black peppercorns
1 tablespoon olive oil
100 g (4 oz) chestnut mushrooms, thinly sliced
2 tablespoons brandy
150 ml (5 fl oz) red wine
1 teaspoon fresh thyme leaves or ¼ teaspoon dried thyme
1 tablespoon redcurrant or cranberry jelly

1 teaspoon balsamic or sherry vinegar
salt and pepper

FOR THE POTATO GALETTES
225g/8 oz potato, coarsely grated
2 tablespoons plain flour
1 tablespoon olive oil
small fresh thyme sprig or whole chives, to garnish

Place the steak on a chopping board and sprinkle generously with the cracked peppercorns, pressing them into the surface of the steak with your fingertips. Brush the steaks with the oil and sprinkle with a little salt. Cook the steaks in a hot frying pan for 3–4 minutes on each side until well browned but still a little pink in the centre. Meanwhile, make the potato galettes: mix together the potato, flour and a little salt. Heat the oil in a separate frying pan and, dividing the potato mixture into two, drop in two small piles of potato; flatten down with a fish slice and cook for 3–4 minutes on each side until crisp and golden. Remove the steaks from the pan, place on a plate and cover to keep warm. Add the mushrooms to the steak pan and stir-fry for a minute or so until beginning to brown. Pour the brandy into the hot pan and carefully ignite. When the flames have died down, stir in the wine, thyme, redcurrant jelly and vinegar and boil for 2–3 minutes, stirring until the jelly dissolves; season to taste. Place the potato galettes on two serving plates and top with the steaks. Spoon round the mushroom gravy, garnish with herbs and serve.

NUTRITION NOTES PER SERVING: calories 597 | protein 37.5 g | carbohydrate 51 g fat 19.2 g | saturated fat 4.45 g | fibre 2.6 g | added sugar 5.2 g | salt 0.3 g

If you don't have a pestle and mortar, place whole black peppercorns in a small, strong plastic bag and bash with a heavy rolling pin.

merry berry christmas crumble

This is my idea of a treat for any day of the week – and it's a great way to use up the left-over mincemeat and cranberries that have been hanging around since Christmas!

SERVES 4   **PREPARATION: 15 MINS | COOKING TIME: 35 MINS**

4 pears or eating apples, cored and sliced
75 g (3 oz) fresh or frozen cranberries
2 tablespoons orange juice
1 banana, thickly sliced
3–4 tablespoons mincemeat
50 g (2 oz) butter, cut into pieces
100 g (4 oz) plain flour
25 g (1 oz) light muscovado sugar
custard, to serve

Preheat the oven to 190°C/375°F/gas 5. Place the pear or apple slices, cranberries and orange juice in a pan, cover and cook over a low heat for 7–8 minutes until the fruit is beginning to soften. Remove from the heat and stir in the banana and mincemeat, then transfer to a pie dish.

Rub the butter into the flour until it resembles fine breadcrumbs, then stir in the sugar. Spoon over the fruit and bake for 20–25 minutes until the topping is golden. Serve immediately with custard.

NUTRITION NOTES PER SERVING: calories 357 | protein 3.5 g | carbohydrate 63.1 g fat 11.8 g | saturated fat 7.15 g | fibre 5.3 g | added sugar 9.7 g | salt 0.33 g

golden sunglazed apricot rice

Flaked rice makes this dessert incredibly quick, as it's so easy to use, and the finished dish is simply gorgeous. For an extra richness, add four tablespoons of cream to the rice while cooking.

SERVES 4   **PREPARATION: 10 MINS | COOKING TIME: 20 MINS**

100 g (4 oz) ready-to-eat dried apricots
50 g (2 oz) sultanas
1 lemon
75 g (3 oz) flaked rice
750 ml (1¼ pints) semi-skimmed milk
50 g (2 oz) caster sugar
8 tablespoons apricot jam
fresh mint sprigs, to decorate

Reserve 4 of the dried apricots, then chop the rest. Mix together the chopped dried apricots and sultanas and set aside. Using a swivel-style vegetable peeler, cut wide strips of rind from the lemon.

Place the lemon-rind strips, rice, milk and sugar in a pan and bring to the boil, then reduce the heat and simmer for 12–15 minutes, stirring often. Stir in the dried fruit, divide between four serving bowls and set aside to cool slightly.

To make the apricot glaze squeeze 1 tablespoon of juice from the lemon into a small pan. Stir in 2 tablespoons of water, then add the jam. Bring to the boil, stirring, until the jam has melted, then immediately remove from the heat. Leave for a few minutes to cool and thicken slightly, then pour over the rice puddings. Decorate each with a dried apricot and a mint sprig.

NUTRITION NOTES PER SERVING: calories 373 | protein 9 g | carbohydrate 82 g
fat 3 g | saturated fat 2 g | fibre 2 g | added sugar 41 g | salt 0.27 g

lemon caramel strawberry nests

If you like the taste of toffee apples, just wait until you taste these sticky summer puddings that are literally assembled in minutes. Go on, get tacky!

SERVES 4 | **PREPARATION: 15 MINS | COOKING TIME: 10 MINS**

250 g (9 oz) mascarpone cheese
150 ml (5 fl oz) single cream
1 tablespoon icing sugar
250 g (9 oz) strawberries, hulled
4 ready-made meringue nests
75 g (3 oz) caster sugar
3 tablespoons fresh lemon juice
2 tablespoons chopped toasted hazelnuts

Beat together the mascarpone cheese, cream and icing sugar until smooth. Reserve four of the strawberries and chop the remainder. Stir the chopped strawberries into the cream mixture and use to fill the meringue baskets. Slice the reserved strawberries and stick the slices into the cream. Place each in the centre of a serving plate.

Gently heat the caster sugar and lemon juice in a heavy-based pan, set over a very low heat, stirring until the sugar dissolves. Increase the heat and allow the mixture to bubble for about 4 minutes until golden – as the mixture cooks, don't stir, but swirl the pan occasionally so it doesn't burn around the edges.

Remove from the heat and add the chopped hazelnuts and a tablespoon of water. Swirl to combine, then immediately pour over the meringue nests and serve.

NUTRITION NOTES PER SERVING: calories 681 | protein 7 g | carbohydrate 76 g fat 41 g | saturated fat 23 g | fibre 1 g | added sugar 67 g | salt 0.34 g

sydney's fruit coconut smoothie

A fruit smoothie is a refreshingly delicious Australian-style summer drink, but it also doubles up well as a silky sauce for these cool fruity puddings.

SERVES 4   **PREPARATION: 15 MINS**

350 g (12 oz) strawberries, halved or sliced
2 nectarines or peaches, stoned and sliced
100 g (4 oz) blueberries or black grapes
1 large banana
120 ml (4 fl oz) fresh orange juice
200 g (7 oz) Greek yogurt
2 tablespoons desiccated coconut, toasted

Mix together the strawberries, nectarines or peaches and blueberries or grapes and divide between four tall glass pudding dishes.

To make the fruit smoothie roughly chop the banana, then place in a food processor or blender with the orange juice and yogurt and process until smooth.

Pour the smoothie over the fruit in the bowls and sprinkle each with toasted desiccated coconut; serve.

NUTRITION NOTES PER SERVING: calories 201 | protein 6 g | carbohydrate 26 g fat 9 g | saturated fat 6 g | fibre 4 g | added sugar none | salt 0.11 g

For a really cool smoothie, peel the banana, wrap in plastic film and place in the freezer for 1–2 hours. Cut the banana in half, place in a food processor or blender with the orange juice and yogurt and process until smooth.

chocolate-orange drizzle fruit

This fruity concoction cries out for a rich drizzle of chocolate, so how could I resist? It's a fantastic finale to any meal.

SERVES 4   PREPARATION: 15 MINS | COOKING TIME: 15 MINS

2 oranges
50 g (2 oz) butter
4 tablespoons light muscovado sugar
2 tablespoons fresh lemon juice
2 pears, peeled, halved and cored
2 apples, peeled, quartered and cored
75 g (3 oz) plain chocolate, broken into pieces
4 tablespoons whipping or double cream

Using a zester, remove the rind from one orange and set aside. Finely grate 1 teaspoon of rind from the second orange and reserve. Using a sharp knife, remove and discard the remaining rind and pith from both oranges, reserving any juices. Slice the fruit thickly.

Melt the butter in a frying pan and add the sugar and stir until dissolved. Stir in the rind from the first orange, the lemon juice, orange slices, pears and apples, and cook for 5 minutes until softened.

Microwave the chocolate on PL9/high for 1½–2 minutes (or set the bowl over a pan of simmering water) until melted. Stir in the teaspoon of orange rind, reserved orange juice and cream.

Divide the fruit between serving bowls, spoon over the juices, and drizzle over the chocolate sauce.

NUTRITION NOTES PER SERVING: calories 459 | protein 3 g | carbohydrate 53 g fat 28 g | saturated fat 17 g | fibre 4 g | added sugar 32 g | salt 0.3 g

scrunched spiced apple cream pie

Forget boring old apple tarts, this spiced-up pie has a brandy-cream layer and a scrunchy, crunchy filo topping . . . delicious!

SERVES 2   PREPARATION: 10 MINS | COOKING TIME: 10 MINS

FOR THE FILLING
50 g (2 oz) butter
1 kg (2¼ lb) dessert apples,
  peeled, cored and sliced
50 g (2 oz) caster sugar
½ teaspoon ground cinnamon
½ teaspoon ground ginger

FOR THE TOPPING
6 sheets filo pastry
25 g (1 oz) melted butter
icing sugar, for dusting
4 tablespoons brandy
1 tablespoon light
  muscovado sugar
150 ml (5 fl oz) double cream

Pre-heat the oven to 220°C/450°F/gas 7.

Heat the butter in a large pan and throw in the apple slices. Sprinkle over the sugar, cinnamon and ginger and cook for 3 minutes, stirring frequently. Cover and cook gently for a further 5 minutes until softened.

Meanwhile, brush the pastry sheets with the melted butter and roughly scrunch up. Place on a baking sheet and dust with icing sugar. Bake for 6–7 minutes until golden brown.

Spoon the apple mixture into a buttered pie dish; keep warm. Swirl the brandy into the pan then stir in the light muscovado sugar and cream and cook for 2–3 minutes, scraping up any residue on the bottom of the pan with a wooden spoon.

Pour the cream sauce over the apple mixture then arrange the scrunched filo on top. Dust with a little extra icing sugar and serve warm.

NUTRITION NOTES PER SERVING: calories 1202 | protein 7 g | carbohydrate 129.7 g
fat 69 g | saturated fat 42.47 g | fibre 7.6 g | added sugar 40.8 g | salt 2.17 g

amazing mango marzipan tartlets

So . . . how do you like your tarts? Oooh, perhaps with plums, or you might prefer apricots. But for me it has to be a nice ripe mango. Believe me, once bitten, forever smitten!

SERVES 4 | **PREPARATION: 10 MINS | COOKING TIME: 15 MINS**

250 g (9 oz) puff pastry
150 g (5 oz) marzipan, cut into 4 x 6 mm (¼ in) thick slices
2 mangoes
4 tablespoons lemon curd
150 ml (5 fl oz) double cream, whipped to soft peaks

Pre-heat the oven to 220°C/425°F/gas 7.

Roll the puff pastry on a lightly floured surface to give a 28 cm (11 in) square. Cut into four equal-sized squares and transfer to a baking sheet. Cut each marzipan slice into two triangles. Place two of the triangles, overlapping slightly, in the centre of each pastry square.

Slice each mango down both sides of its central stone. Peel, then make lengthways cuts through each piece of mango, almost to the end. Gently press down on the mango to fan out the slices.

Place one mango fan, flat-side down, on the centre of each pastry square then spread 1 tablespoon of lemon curd over each piece of mango. Bake for 12–15 minutes until the pastry is risen and golden.

Meanwhile, remove any remaining flesh from around the mango stones and chop finely; stir into the whipped cream. Serve the tarts warm with a dollop of the mango cream.

NUTRITION NOTES PER SERVING: calories 638 | protein 6.8 g | carbohydrate 69.5 g fat 39 g | saturated fat 11.72 g | fibre 2.7 g | added sugar 24.5 g | salt 0.57 g

mango cranberry nut crumble

I don't know anyone who can resist the tempting taste of a mouthwatering crumble, so here's one that keeps that tradition going. Canned mango is a great store-cupboard standby. Its sweet and juicy flesh works brilliantly in this tropical nut crumble.

SERVES 4 | PREPARATION: 10 MINS | COOKING TIME: 35 MINS

25 g (1 oz) dried or ready-to-eat packet cranberries
grated rind and juice of 1 large orange
150 g (5 oz) plain flour
100 g (4 oz) butter, chilled and diced
75 g (3 oz) caster sugar
25 g (1 oz) flaked almonds, roughly chopped
½ teaspoon ground mixed spice
400 g (14 oz) can mango slices in syrup, drained
custard or cream, to serve

Pre-heat the oven to 190°C/375°F/gas 5.

Place the cranberries and orange juice in a small pan and gently bring to the boil; remove from the heat and set aside for 5 minutes.

Meanwhile, place the flour and butter in a large bowl, then, using the fingertips, rub together until the mixture resembles coarse breadcrumbs. Stir in the caster sugar, almonds and mixed spice.

Stir together the cranberries and orange juice and mix with the mango slices and the orange rind. Spoon the mixture into a buttered pie dish and sprinkle over the crumble. Bake in the oven for 25–30 minutes until golden brown. Serve with hot custard or pouring cream.

NUTRITION NOTES PER SERVING: calories 498 | protein 5.4 g | carbohydrate 68.5 g
fat 24.4 g | saturated fat 13.35 g | fibre 2.2 g | added sugar 27.2 g | salt 0.49 g

DESSERTS

terrific toffee-choc cake pudding

Once again it's time to overindulge – that's if you consider a pudding like this a naughty treat. It's simply heavenly and delicious, so just slap it on those thighs, as me wife would say.

SERVES 4 | PREPARATION: 10 MINS | COOKING TIME: 10 MINS

175 g (6 oz) block ready-made chocolate or marble cake
2 tablespoons brandy (optional)
50 g (2 oz) butter, plus extra for melting
75 g (3 oz) light muscovado sugar
3 tablespoons golden syrup
150 ml (5 fl oz) double cream
25 g (1 oz) toasted hazelnuts, chopped
1 banana, sliced
rind and juice of 1 small orange
icing sugar and mint sprigs, to decorate

Preheat the oven to 200°C/400°F/gas 6.

Cut the cake into 1 cm (½ in) thick slices. Place in a small, shallow ovenproof dish and drizzle over the brandy, if using.

Place 50 g (2 oz) of the butter in a small pan with the sugar and golden syrup. Stir over a low heat until the butter is melted and the sugar dissolved. Stir in the cream and remove from the heat. Pour the sauce over the cake and sprinkle with the nuts. Bake for 10 minutes until the sauce is bubbling.

Meanwhile, heat a small knob of butter in a small frying pan. Add the banana slices and orange rind and cook briefly until golden. Pour in the orange juice and remove from the heat.

Place a slice of cake on each serving plate. Spoon over some sauce, top with banana slices, dust with icing sugar and decorate each with a mint sprig.

NUTRITION NOTES PER SERVING: calories 688 | protein 5 g | carbohydrate 69 g
fat 44 g | saturated fat 25 g | fibre 1 g | added sugar 51 g | salt 0.9 g

DESSERTS

178

zapped lemon
curd pudding

**The microwave is an amazing way to cook light and fluffy puddings
in no time at all. This tangy lemon pud can be served with hot custard or
whipped cinnamon cream.**

SERVES 4   **PREPARATION: 5 MINS | COOKING TIME: 6 MINS**

100 g (4 oz) butter
100 g (4 oz) caster sugar
100 g (4 oz) self-raising flour
2 eggs, beaten
grated rind of 1 lemon
4 tablespoons lemon curd
custard or whipped cinnamon cream, to serve
fresh mint springs, to garnish

Place the butter, sugar, flour, eggs and lemon rind in a food processor and
whizz together until well blended.

Drop a tablespoon of lemon curd into the base of four buttered, heatproof
teacups. Spoon the sponge mixture on top; cover with micro-film and microwave
individually on PL9/high for 1½ minutes until risen and cooked through. Rest for
1 minute before serving.

Pour the custard on top of each sponge and serve in the cup or turn out onto
small plates and pour the custard round the base of each. Alternatively, whip
some double cream with a pinch of cinnamon and put a dollop on top of each
pudding. Spike with a mint sprig and serve.

NUTRITION NOTES PER SERVING: calories 444 | protein 5.6 g | carbohydrate 54.6 g
fat 24.2 g | saturated fat 13.8 g | fibre 0.8 g | added sugar 32.3 g | salt 0.82 g

DESSERTS

179

caramel alaskas

This glamorous dessert is my own up-market version of the classic baked Alaska, with the light muscovado sugar in the meringue adding a delicious caramel flavour. At Christmas time, why not try replacing the Madeira cake with Christmas cake?

SERVES 4 **PREPARATION: 15 MINS | COOKING TIME: 5 MINS**

3–4 tablespoons ground almonds
4 scoops raspberry ripple or vanilla ice cream
4 x 1 cm (½ in) thick square Madeira cake slices
2–3 tablespoons brandy
9–12 mandarin segments
3 egg whites
175 g (6 oz) light muscovado sugar
icing sugar, for dusting

Place the almonds on a plate and roll the ice cream scoops in them. Place on a baking sheet and open freeze for 30 minutes until firm.

Place the cake slices well apart on a baking sheet. Drizzle with brandy and arrange the mandarin segments end-to-end to make a ring in the centre of each slice. Place an almond-covered ice-cream scoop in the middle of each ring. Return to the freezer while you make the meringue.

Pre-heat the oven to 230°C/450°F/gas 8. Place the egg whites in a clean, grease-free bowl. Whisk in the sugar, a tablespoon at a time, whisking thoroughly after each addition until the mixture forms soft peaks. Spoon the meringue over the ice cream and spread to cover. Bake for about 5 minutes until the meringue starts to brown. Transfer to the serving plates, dust with icing sugar and serve immediately.

NUTRITION NOTES PER SERVING: calories 477 | protein 8.6 g | carbohydrate 73.7 g
fat 16.6 g | saturated fat 5.65 g | fibre 1.4 g | added sugar 62.4 g | salt 0.41 g

crackingly fruity mount vesuvius

What a spectacular dessert! Eat this and the earth really will move!

SERVES 4 | **PREPARATION: 15 MINS | COOKING TIME: 5 MINS**

250 g (9 oz) mixed fruit such as strawberries, mango and grapes, cut into chunks
1 tablespoon caster sugar
2 tablespoons white rum
50 g (2 oz) amaretti or almond macaroons

FOR THE CARAMEL
100 g (4 oz) caster sugar
juice of 1 lemon

FOR THE TOPPING
250 g (9 oz) mascarpone cheese
2 tablespoons white rum
2 tablespoons icing sugar
grated rind of 1 lemon
mint sprigs, to serve

Place the fruit, caster sugar and rum in a large bowl and mix well together; set aside for 5 minutes.

For the caramel, place the sugar, lemon juice and a splash of water in a small pan. Heat gently, stirring until the sugar dissolves, then raise the heat and boil rapidly, without stirring, until golden.

Meanwhile, for the topping, mix together the mascarpone, rum, icing sugar and lemon rind.

Arrange the biscuits in the base of four individual dishes and spoon over the fruit mixture. Spoon the flavoured mascarpone on top of the fruit, shaping it to a tall peak in the centre.

Pour caramel over the top of each, set aside for a minute or two until the caramel sets, then serve immediately, decorated with mint sprigs.

NUTRITION NOTES PER SERVING: calories 508 | protein 3.2 g | carbohydrate 47 g
fat 31.5 g | saturated fat 18.2 g | fibre 1.3 g | added sugar 28.9 g | salt 0.18 g

DESSERTS

choco-nana brandy snaps

Chocolate and banana whip up with fromage frais to make a yummy filling for ready-made brandy snaps – ideal for a quick dessert. For an attractive garnish slice an unskinned banana, dust liberally with icing sugar and pop under a hot grill until caramelized and golden.

SERVES 4 | **PREPARATION: 5 MINS | COOKING TIME: 5 MINS**

100 g (4 oz) dark chocolate
1 large banana, roughly chopped
200 g (7 oz) fromage frais
1 tablespoon icing sugar, plus extra, to dust
a few drops of vanilla extract
25 g (1 oz) flaked or chopped hazelnuts, toasted
8 brandy snaps
1 extra banana for garnish (optional)

Break the chocolate into a heatproof bowl and microwave on PL9/high for 1½–2 minutes, or sit over a pan of simmering water, stirring occasionally, until melted.

Place the banana in a food processor and whizz to make a smooth purée. Add the fromage frais, icing sugar and vanilla extract and blend again, then with the motor running, slowly drizzle in the chocolate until smooth and well blended.

Stir the hazelnuts into the mixture then spoon into a piping bag. Pipe the filling into the brandy snaps, dust with icing sugar, garnish with banana if using, and serve.

NUTRITION NOTES PER SERVING: calories 404 | protein 6.6 g | carbohydrate 49.8 g fat 21 g | saturated fat 10.83 g | fibre 1 g | added sugar 32.4 g | salt 0.24 g

citrus banana soufflé omelette

This sweet omelette is filled with yummy banana custard – I've served my banana custard cold, but if you want to, warm it gently in a small pan. Please do remember to grate only the rind, not the white pith of the lemon, which is bitter.

SERVES 2   **PREPARATION: 10 MINS | COOKING TIME: 5 MINS**

3 eggs, separated
1 tablespoon light muscovado sugar
a few drops of vanilla extract
2 large bananas, roughly mashed
grated rind of 1 lemon
100 ml (3½ fl oz) ready-made custard
a knob of butter
icing sugar, to dust

Stir together the egg yolks, light muscovado sugar and vanilla extract and set aside. Roughly mash the bananas, add the lemon rind and fold together with the custard.

In a large bowl whisk the egg whites until stiff, then gently fold in the egg yolk mixture. Pre-heat the grill to high.

Heat the butter in a 20 cm (8 in) frying pan and pour in the soufflé mixture; cook for 2–3 minutes until the underside is golden, then place under a hot grill for 1–2 minutes until puffed and golden.

Spoon the banana custard on top of the soufflé and fold in half to enclose the filling. Slide onto a plate, cut in half and dust liberally with icing sugar; serve immediately.

NUTRITION NOTES PER SERVING: calories 362 | protein 12.7 g | carbohydrate 47.3 g fat 14.8 g | saturated fat 6.41 g | fibre 1.3 g | added sugar 14 g | salt 0.47 g

---

If you're feeling really fancy, heat a skewer in a gas flame and press down on top of the icing-sugar dusted soufflé – it will caramelize the sugar immediately, giving an attractive branding mark, which can be repeated to make a lattice or criss-cross effect.

DESSERTS

titillating tarty rhuby souflette

Try my puffy tarty souflette – it's packed full of spiced juicy fruit and really captures the eyes and the tastebuds.

SERVES 4	PREPARATION: 10 MINS | COOKING TIME: 10 MINS

250 g (9 oz) rhubarb, cut into 2.5 cm (1 in) pieces
1 tablespoon orange juice or water
4 tablespoons caster sugar
a good pinch of mixed spice
100 g (4 oz) strawberries, sliced
3 eggs, separated
1 teaspoon finely grated orange rind
a knob of butter
icing sugar, for dusting
crème fraîche, to serve

Place the rhubarb, orange juice or water, 3 tablespoons of the sugar and the mixed spice in a pan and bring to the boil; simmer for 4 minutes until tender and thickened. Stir in the strawberries and set aside.

Beat the egg yolks and remaining sugar until pale, then stir in the orange rind. In a separate bowl, whisk the egg whites until stiff. Fold the egg yolks carefully into the whites.

Pre-heat the grill to medium. Melt the butter in a 23 cm (9 in) frying pan and spoon in the egg mixture so it covers the base. Cook over a gentle heat for a few minutes until golden underneath and beginning to set, then grill for 1 minute until golden and puffy.

Slide the souflette onto a serving plate and spoon some of the fruit and sauce over one half. Fold over and dust liberally with icing sugar. Serve in wedges with extra fruit and a dollop of crème fraîche on the side.

NUTRITION NOTES PER SERVING: calories 170 \| protein 5.5 g \| carbohydrate 24.6 g
fat 6.2 g \| saturated fat 2.44 g \| fibre 1.2 g \| added sugar 22.3 g \| salt 0.19 g

DESSERTS

silvana's orange tagliatelle suzette

This version of the classic French dish Crêpes Suzette is so wonderfully satisfying and is a delightful way to finish a meal, perhaps with a glass of dessert wine.

SERVES 4 | **PREPARATION: 10 MINS | COOKING TIME: 15 MINS**

100 g (4 oz) plain flour
¼ teaspoon salt
1 egg, beaten
25 g (1 oz) melted butter
250 ml (8 fl oz) milk
sunflower oil, for frying
40 g (1½ oz) unsalted butter
2 tablespoons caster sugar, plus 1 teaspoon
grated rind and juice of 2 oranges
2 tablespoons brandy
cream, to serve

Sieve the flour and salt into a bowl. Make a well in the centre and pour in the egg, butter and half the milk. Whisk until smooth, then gradually whisk in the remaining milk to give a smooth batter.

Heat a little oil in an 18 cm (7 in) pancake or frying pan and swirl in 2 tablespoons of the batter; cook for a minute or so until golden then flip and cook for a further 30 seconds. Repeat to make eight pancakes. Lay the pancakes on top of each other, then roll up. Cut into 1 cm (½ in) wide strips.

Heat the butter in a large frying pan with the 2 tablespoons of caster sugar and the orange juice and rind, stirring until the sugar dissolves. Toss in the pancake strips and gently heat through.

Push the pancakes to one side of the pan and increase the heat. Sprinkle the remaining teaspoon of caster sugar onto the space in the pan and, when the sugar begins to melt and bubble, pour over the brandy; carefully ignite. Allow the flames to subside then serve immediately with cream.

NUTRITION NOTES PER SERVING: calories 384 | protein 6.1 g | carbohydrate 36.5 g fat 22.9 g | saturated fat 11.12 g | fibre 0.8 g | added sugar 11.8 g | salt 0.56 g

index

Italic type indicates illustrations

acknowledgements

A big thank you goes to Silvana Franco for testing the recipes along with Bridget Colvin and Annalisa Aldridge; also to Angela Nilsen at *Good Food Magazine* for her early inspiration whilst I created the recipes; to my producer Caroline Officer and assistant producer Orla Broderick for all their hard work, energy and enthusiasm; to my researcher Sarah Williams (what a cracking job).

Thanks also to Bazal Productions and all at BBC television and BBC Books, especially my editor Nicky Copeland; to my agent 'Come on the Blues' Jerry Hicks, Sarah Dolkin and, of course, to my delightful wife Clare and our adorable kids Jimmy and Madeleine.